EASY EVERYDAY
Lighter dinners

Woman's Day

EASY EVERYDAY
Lighter dinners

Healthy, family-friendly mains, sides and desserts

by Kate Merker and the editors of *Woman's Day*

HEARST BOOKS

New York

Foreword

Here's what I hear most often when I ask *Woman's Day* readers about healthy meals:

"Healthy? My family won't touch it."

"Healthy ingredients are too expensive."

"I don't have time to cook special meals."

"Yuck!" (OK, that's a quote from my older daughter, who basically hates anything green.)

It's no wonder that the idea of cooking nutritious meals drives many of us straight to the frozen pizza aisle. It just seems, well, hard. And who needs hard at the end of a long day?

That's where our new cookbook comes in. These pages are proof that healthy meals can be quick and easy to cook, and delicious as well. We've gathered a selection of recipes from our popular Easy Everyday section, as well as special features. These dishes don't call for fancy (or expensive) ingredients—just wholesome foods you can buy at your local supermarket. We've paid close attention to fat and calories, but also added recipes that sneak in lean proteins, whole grains, antioxidant-packed fruits and vegetables and other nutritional musts that keep your body strong. Your family won't even taste the difference.

So resist the siren call of frozen dinners and try out these recipes. We've been loving them in my household (yes, even my vegetable-averse child). Enjoy!

Susan

Susan Spencer
EDITOR-IN-CHIEF, *WOMAN'S DAY*

Introduction

Growing up, my family had a few dinnertime rules:

1. We ate dinner together.

2. Salad was served at every meal (my brother and I had the choice of eating it before the main dish, which was my father's preference, or after, which was my mother's).

3. We had to try everything on the table (even the vegetables).

4. We ate what was served for dinner—no substitutions.

5. Monday nights we had ravioli.

These rules taught me that balance is key, and that's something we promote every month in *Woman's Day*. In my home, this still holds true (although ravioli is now fair game any night of the week).

I know that life is busy and getting dinner on the table can be the most hectic part of the day. So we filled this book with easy recipes that you can incorporate into your weekly rotation, and dishes you can whip up on the fly when you don't have a plan. You'll never hear "This again!" again.

Our recipes are lower in fat and calories, but this is not a book of "diet" food. It's food that can fill up your family and that you can feel good about serving at the same time. So, whether you are in search of a comforting pasta dish (try the Vegetable lasagna on page 39) or a 20-minute meal (Cajun shrimp, spinach and grits on page 25 is a favorite), we have it. You'll also notice a ♥ icon, which marks every recipe that meets our heart-healthy criteria for fat, saturated fat, cholesterol and sodium. I am proud to say that 53 recipes in this cookbook met this standard.

There are dozens of complete meal options to choose from, but if you are just looking for a side dish to pair with a quick sautéed chicken breast we have those too. And what meal doesn't feel complete without dessert? Try any one of the sweet treats in the last chapter (one of my favorites, the Banana oat cookies on page 131).

Whether you have ravioli Mondays, taco Tuesdays or pizza Fridays, the WD food team wishes you many wonderful (and healthy!) meals with your family.

Happy cooking,

Kate

Kate Merker
FOOD & NUTRITION DIRECTOR, *WOMAN'S DAY*

p64

p18

p88

p99

Main Courses

Healthier weeknight eating just got easier. Whether you're looking for a hearty one-pot meal or a fresh no-cook option, you'll find it in here.

Turkey meatballs

ACTIVE 35 MIN • **TOTAL** 50 MIN • **SERVES** 6 • **COST PER SERVING** $2.04

- 1 Tbsp olive oil
- 1 medium onion, finely chopped

  Kosher salt and pepper
- ½ cup fresh flat-leaf parsley, chopped
- 8 oz mushrooms, finely chopped
- 2 cloves garlic, finely chopped
- 1 Tbsp Dijon mustard
- ¼ cup quick-cooking oats
- 2 tsp fresh thyme
- 1¼ lb ground turkey breast or extra-lean ground turkey
- 2 Tbsp grated Parmesan
- 2 cups low-sodium marinara sauce

  Green salad, for serving

1 Heat oven to 425°F. Heat the oil in a medium skillet over medium heat. Add the onion, season with ¼ tsp each salt and pepper and cook, covered, stirring occasionally, until tender, 6 to 8 minutes; stir in the parsley.

2 Add the mushrooms and garlic and cook, stirring occasionally, until the mushrooms are tender and their liquid is nearly evaporated, 4 to 5 minutes.

3 Meanwhile, in a large bowl, whisk together the mustard, 2 Tbsp water and ¼ tsp each salt and pepper. Stir in the oats and thyme. Add the turkey, sprinkle with the Parmesan and mix to combine.

4 Fold in the mushroom mixture. Form the mixture into 24 balls and place on a foil-lined baking sheet. Bake until cooked through, 12 to 15 minutes.

5 Warm the marinara sauce in a large skillet. Toss the meatballs in the sauce to coat. Serve with a salad, if desired.

♥ **PER SERVING** 230 CAL, 4.5 G FAT (1 G SAT FAT), 63 MG CHOL, 357 MG SOD, 26 G PRO, 12 G CAR, 2 G FIBER

Make ahead » The cooked meatballs and sauce can be frozen for up to 2 months. Thaw in the refrigerator, then warm in a saucepan, covered, stirring occasionally, over medium heat.

Steak with herbed potatoes

ACTIVE 25 MIN • **TOTAL** 25 MIN • **SERVES** 4 • **COST PER SERVING** $3.10

1 lb small red new potatoes (about 16)

Kosher salt and pepper

3 Tbsp olive oil

4 small steaks (such as sirloin, top round or newport; about 1½ lb total), trimmed

2 scallions, thinly sliced

¼ cup fresh dill, roughly chopped

2 Tbsp white wine vinegar

1 oz feta, crumbled

1 Place the potatoes in a large pot, add enough cold water to cover and bring to a boil. Add 2 tsp salt, reduce heat and simmer until just tender, 15 to 18 minutes. Drain and run under cold water to cool. Cut the potatoes in half.

2 While the potatoes are cooking, heat 1 Tbsp oil in a large skillet over medium-high heat. Season the steaks with ½ tsp each salt and pepper and cook to desired doneness, 4 to 5 minutes per side for medium-rare.

3 In a large bowl, combine the scallions, dill, vinegar, remaining 2 Tbsp oil and ½ tsp each salt and pepper. Add the potatoes and toss to coat. Fold in the feta and serve with the steak.

♥ **PER SERVING** 384 CAL, 16 G FAT (4 G SAT FAT), 89 MG CHOL, 788 MG SOD, 41 G PRO, 20 G CAR, 3 G FIBER

Use up the dill » For a quick dip for vegetables or a tasty sandwich spread, whisk together 1 cup lowfat Greek yogurt, 2 Tbsp fresh lemon juice, 1 Tbsp prepared horseradish and ¼ tsp each salt and pepper in a medium bowl. Fold in ¼ cup fresh dill (chopped) and 2 scallions (finely chopped).

Roasted pork and cabbage with apricot relish

ACTIVE 15 MIN • **TOTAL** 30 MIN • **SERVES** 4
COST PER SERVING $2.95

3	Tbsp olive oil
1	1¼-lb pork tenderloin
	Kosher salt and pepper
½	head green cabbage (about 1½ lb), cored and sliced
1	medium red onion, sliced
1½	cups dried apricots, quartered
3	Tbsp fresh lemon juice
3	Tbsp brown sugar
2	Tbsp Dijon mustard
2	scallions, chopped

❶ Heat oven to 425°F. Heat 1 Tbsp oil in a large skillet over medium-high heat. Season the pork with ½ tsp each salt and pepper and cook, turning occasionally, until browned, 6 to 8 minutes.

❷ Meanwhile, on a large rimmed baking sheet, toss together the cabbage, onion, remaining 2 Tbsp oil, ½ tsp salt and ¼ tsp pepper. Push the cabbage mixture toward the edges of the pan to make space for the pork. Transfer the pork to the baking sheet and roast until the internal temperature reaches 145°F, 10 to 12 minutes. Let the pork rest for 5 minutes before slicing.

❸ While the pork cooks, in a small saucepan, combine the apricots, lemon juice, sugar, mustard, 1¼ cups water, ¼ tsp salt and ⅛ tsp pepper and bring to a boil. Reduce heat and simmer, stirring occasionally, until the liquid slightly thickens and becomes syrupy, 10 to 12 minutes. Fold in the scallions. Serve with the pork and cabbage.

PER SERVING 457 CAL, 14 G FAT (3 G SAT FAT), 78 MG CHOL, 859 MG SOD, 31 G PRO, 55 G CAR, 7 G FIBER

Switch it up » The apricot relish is also great served with seared chicken or white fish. For extra crunch, stir chopped toasted almonds into the relish before serving.

Roasted shrimp scampi

ACTIVE 5 MIN • **TOTAL** 20 MIN • **SERVES** 4
COST PER SERVING $3.38

8	oz linguine
1½	lb large peeled and deveined shrimp
2	Tbsp olive oil
6	cloves garlic, thinly sliced
½	cup fresh flat-leaf parsley, roughly chopped
½	cup small sweet red cherry peppers, quartered
¼	cup dry white wine
	Kosher salt and pepper

1 Heat oven to 425°F. Cook the pasta according to package directions.

2 Meanwhile, in a large baking dish, toss the shrimp, oil, garlic, parsley, cherry peppers, wine, ½ tsp salt and ¼ tsp pepper. Roast until the shrimp are opaque throughout, 12 to 15 minutes. Serve with the pasta.

PER SERVING 398 CAL, 9 G FAT (1 G SAT FAT), 214 MG CHOL, 1,213 MG SOD, 31 G PRO, 46 G CAR, 2 G FIBER

Use up the sweet red cherry peppers »
Make a tangy salsa: Toss together ¼ cup chopped sweet red cherry peppers, ½ red onion (finely chopped), 1 cup grape tomatoes (halved) and ½ cup chopped cilantro. Serve with broiled steak or fish.

Grilled chicken Caesar salad

ACTIVE 15 MIN • **TOTAL** 25 MIN • **SERVES** 4 • **COST PER SERVING** $2.12

- 2 Tbsp fresh lemon juice
- 2 tsp Dijon mustard
- ¼ tsp Worcestershire sauce
- 2 Tbsp grated Parmesan, plus more for serving
- 4 Tbsp olive oil
- Kosher salt and pepper
- 1 medium red onion, cut into ¼-in.-thick wedges
- 2 thick slices country bread
- 4 6-oz boneless, skinless chicken breasts
- 1 small head romaine, sliced crosswise into ½-in.-wide strips (about 8 cups)

❶ Heat grill to medium-high. In a large bowl, whisk together the lemon juice, mustard, Worcestershire, Parmesan, 2 Tbsp oil and ¼ tsp each salt and pepper; set aside.

❷ Brush the onion with 1 Tbsp oil and season with ¼ tsp each salt and pepper. Brush the bread with 2 tsp oil. Brush the chicken with the remaining 1 tsp oil and season with ½ tsp each salt and pepper.

❸ Grill the chicken and onions until the chicken is cooked through and the onions are just tender, 5 to 6 minutes per side. Grill the bread until toasted and slightly charred, 1 to 2 minutes per side.

❹ Cut the bread into 1-in. pieces. Toss the romaine, onions and bread with the dressing. Serve with the chicken (sliced, if desired) and sprinkle with additional Parmesan, if desired.

PER SERVING 387 CAL, 19 G FAT (3 G SAT FAT), 96 MG CHOL, 775 MG SOD, 38 G PRO, 15 G CAR, 3 G FIBER

Top it off » For extra-flavorful croutons, rub the grilled bread slices with garlic before cutting them into pieces.

Quick braised red cabbage and lentils with seared cod

ACTIVE 25 MIN • **TOTAL** 25 MIN • **SERVES** 4 • **COST PER SERVING** $3.98

2	Tbsp olive oil
1	large onion, finely chopped
2	tsp caraway seeds
	Kosher salt and pepper
½	small head red cabbage (about 1 lb), cored and chopped
¼	cup balsamic vinegar
2	tsp orange zest plus ¼ cup juice
½	cup golden raisins
1	15-oz can low-sodium lentils, rinsed
4	6-oz skinless cod fillets
	Fresh flat-leaf parsley, for serving

1 Heat 1 Tbsp oil in a large skillet over medium heat. Add the onion, sprinkle with the caraway and ½ tsp each salt and pepper and cook, covered, stirring occasionally, for 6 minutes. Uncover and continue cooking until the onions are beginning to brown around the edges, 4 to 5 minutes more.

2 Add the cabbage and cook, stirring occasionally, for 4 minutes. Add the vinegar and 2 Tbsp water and simmer until nearly all of the liquid has evaporated, about 3 minutes.

3 Stir in the orange juice and zest. Add the raisins and lentils and toss to combine. Cook until the lentils are heated through and the cabbage is just tender, 3 to 4 minutes more.

4 While the cabbage is cooking, heat the remaining Tbsp oil in a separate large skillet over medium heat. Season the cod with ¼ tsp each salt and pepper and cook until golden brown and opaque throughout, 3 to 4 minutes per side. Toss the cabbage with the parsley, if desired, and serve with the fish.

♥ **PER SERVING** 382 CAL, 6.5 G FAT (1 G SAT FAT), 65 MG CHOL, 558 MG SOD, 36 G PRO, 46 G CAR, 11 G FIBER

Switch it up » To make this into a hearty vegetarian meal, omit the fish and cook one 16-oz pkg potato and onion pierogies according to package directions. If pan-frying, make sure to use olive oil and not butter.

Chicken cutlets with spring green salad

ACTIVE 10 MIN • **TOTAL** 20 MIN • **SERVES** 4
COST PER SERVING $2.43

3	Tbsp olive oil, plus more if needed
8	small chicken cutlets (about 1½ lb)
	Kosher salt and pepper
1	Tbsp white wine vinegar
2	bunches watercress or arugula
6	radishes, thinly sliced
1	cup frozen edamame, thawed
½	small red onion, thinly sliced

1 Heat 1 Tbsp oil in a large skillet over medium-high heat. Season the chicken with ½ tsp salt and ¼ tsp pepper. Working in two batches, cook the chicken until browned and cooked through, 2 to 3 minutes per side (adding more oil to the skillet if needed); transfer to plates.

2 In a large bowl, whisk together the vinegar, the remaining 2 Tbsp oil and ½ tsp each salt and pepper. Add the watercress, radishes, edamame and onion and toss to combine. Serve with the chicken.

♥ PER SERVING 262 CAL, 12 G FAT (2 G SAT FAT), 89 MG CHOL, 562 MG SOD, 35 G PRO, 5 G CAR, 2 G FIBER

Use up the edamame » For a quick dip, purée 1 cup each thawed edamame and peas, ½ cup ricotta cheese, ¼ cup grated Parmesan, 2 Tbsp each fresh lemon juice and olive oil, and ½ tsp each salt and pepper.

Pork chops with apricot rice

ACTIVE 15 MIN • **TOTAL** 25 MIN • **SERVES** 4
COST PER SERVING $2.57

1	cup long-grain white rice
¼	cup dried apricots (about 8), chopped
2	scallions, thinly sliced
1	Tbsp olive oil
4	bone-in pork chops (about 1-in. thick)
	Kosher salt and pepper
½	cup dry white wine
¼	cup apricot jam

1 Cook the rice according to package directions, adding the apricots to the saucepan along with the rice. Fluff with a fork and fold in the scallions.

2 Meanwhile, heat the oil in a large skillet over medium heat. Season the pork with ½ tsp each salt and pepper and cook until golden brown and cooked through, 6 to 8 minutes per side. Transfer to plates.

3 Add the wine to the skillet and cook, scraping up any brown bits, for 1 minute. Whisk in the apricot jam and cook until melted. Serve over the pork chops with the rice.

♥ **PER SERVING** 396 CAL, 7 G FAT (2 G SAT FAT), 65 MG CHOL, 328 MG SOD, 29 G PRO, 54 G CAR, 1 G FIBER

Cook's tip » The technique used to make the sauce in this recipe—adding liquid to a hot pan that meat (or vegetables or fish) has been sautéed in, then scraping up the brown bits left on the pan—is called deglazing. Try it with stock or apple cider.

Cajun shrimp, spinach and grits

ACTIVE 20 MIN • **TOTAL** 20 MIN • **SERVES** 4 • **COST PER SERVING** $3.87

1 cup quick-cooking grits

2 Tbsp olive oil

1½ lb large peeled and deveined shrimp

2 tsp Cajun or blackening seasoning (no salt added)

Kosher salt and pepper

2 Tbsp fresh lime juice

2 cloves garlic, thinly sliced

1 cup frozen corn, thawed

1 bunch spinach, thick stems discarded

❶ Cook the grits according to package directions.

❷ Meanwhile, heat 1 Tbsp oil in a large skillet over medium-high heat. Season the shrimp with the Cajun seasoning and ¼ tsp salt and cook for 2 minutes. Turn and cook until opaque throughout, 1 to 2 minutes more. Remove the skillet from the heat, add the lime juice and toss to coat. Transfer to a plate.

❸ Wipe out the skillet and heat the remaining Tbsp oil over medium heat. Add the garlic and cook, stirring, until golden brown, 1 to 2 minutes. Add the corn and cook until heated through.

❹ Add the spinach and ¼ tsp each salt and pepper and cook, tossing, for 1 minute. Return the shrimp to the skillet and toss to combine. Serve over the grits.

PER SERVING 384 CAL, 9 G FAT (1 G SAT FAT), 214 MG CHOL, 452 MG SOD, 29 G PRO, 44 G CAR, 4 G FIBER

Switch it up » Turn this recipe into a hearty vegetarian meal. Omit the shrimp and brush 4 medium portobello mushrooms with olive oil then sprinkle with the Cajun seasoning. Broil until tender, about 3 minutes per side. Cut into 1-in. pieces and toss with the lime juice. Serve on top of the grits and spinach mixture.

Coconut chicken curry

ACTIVE 20 MIN • **TOTAL** 25 MIN • **SERVES** 4 • **COST PER SERVING** $1.76

1	cup long-grain white rice
1	Tbsp olive oil
1½	lb boneless, skinless chicken breasts, sliced ¼ in. thick
1	small onion, chopped
3	cloves garlic, finely chopped
1	Tbsp ground ginger
1	small apple, cut into ½-in. pieces
¼	cup golden raisins
1	Tbsp curry powder
1	cup light coconut milk
1	cup low-sodium chicken broth
	Chopped cilantro, for serving

❶ Cook the rice according to package directions.

❷ Meanwhile, heat the oil in a large nonstick skillet over medium heat. Add the chicken and onion and cook, stirring occasionally, until the chicken is just beginning to brown, 5 to 6 minutes.

❸ Add the garlic and ginger and cook, stirring, for 1 minute. Add the apple and raisins, sprinkle with the curry powder and cook, tossing, for 1 minute.

❹ Stir in the coconut milk, then the broth and simmer, covered, until the chicken is cooked through and the apples and onions are tender, about 5 minutes. Serve over the rice and top with cilantro, if desired.

PER SERVING 530 CAL, 12.5 G FAT (5 G SAT FAT), 109 MG CHOL, 226 MG SOD, 43 G PRO, 59 G CAR, 3 G FIBER

Love your leftovers » Split pita bread in half and spoon leftover chicken curry inside along with baby spinach or arugula and thinly sliced red onion.

Seared salmon with potatoes, cabbage and horseradish vinaigrette

ACTIVE 25 MIN • **TOTAL** 25 MIN • **SERVES** 4
COST PER SERVING $3.09

- 1 lb red new potatoes (about 12)
   Kosher salt and pepper
- ½ small head Savoy cabbage, sliced
- 4 scallions, sliced
- 1 Tbsp prepared horseradish
- 1 Tbsp white wine vinegar
- 2 Tbsp plus 1 tsp olive oil
- 1 1¼-lb piece skinless salmon fillet, cut into 4 pieces

1 Place the potatoes in a medium saucepan. Add enough cold water to cover and bring to a boil. Add 1 tsp salt, reduce heat and simmer for 10 minutes.

2 Add the cabbage and simmer until the potatoes and cabbage are just tender, 5 to 8 minutes more. Drain and run under cold water to cool slightly. Cut the potatoes in half. Transfer the cabbage and potatoes to plates.

3 Meanwhile, in a small bowl, combine the scallions, horseradish, vinegar, 2 Tbsp oil, ¼ tsp salt and ⅛ tsp pepper.

4 Heat the remaining tsp oil in a large nonstick skillet over medium-high heat. Season the salmon with ½ tsp salt and ¼ tsp pepper, and cook until opaque throughout, 3 to 4 minutes per side. Serve the salmon with the potatoes and cabbage, and drizzle with the vinaigrette.

♥ **PER SERVING** 416 CAL, 18 G FAT (3 G SAT FAT), 90 MG CHOL, 524 MG SOD, 36 G PRO, 24 G CAR, 3 G FIBER

Cook's tip » The horseradish vinaigrette is a great dressing for any kind of protein. Or try tossing it with mixed greens or cooked cut potatoes for a zippy salad.

Butternut squash soup

ACTIVE 30 MIN • **TOTAL** 30 MIN • **SERVES** 4
COST PER SERVING 63¢

- 2 Tbsp olive oil
- 1 large onion, chopped
  Kosher salt and pepper
- 2 medium carrots, chopped
- ½ medium butternut squash (about 1½ lb), cut into ¼-in. pieces
- 6 cups water or low-sodium chicken broth
- 2 sprigs fresh rosemary
- ½ small baguette, sliced
- 2 oz Cheddar, coarsely grated
- 2 scallions, thinly sliced
  Crumbled bacon, for serving

1 Heat the oil in a large pot over medium heat. Add the onion, season with ½ tsp salt and ¼ tsp pepper and cook, covered, stirring occasionally, for 6 minutes.

2 Add the carrots and squash and cook, covered, stirring occasionally, for 5 minutes. Add the water and rosemary and bring to a boil. Reduce heat and simmer until the vegetables are tender, 12 to 15 minutes.

3 Heat the broiler. Remove and discard the rosemary. Using an immersion blender (or a standard blender, working in batches), purée the soup.

4 Place the bread on a foil-lined, broiler-proof rimmed baking sheet. Sprinkle with the cheese and broil until the cheese melts, 1 to 2 minutes. Top the soup with the scallions and bacon, if desired and serve with the cheesy toasts.

PER SERVING 286 CAL, 15 G FAT (3.5 G SAT FAT), 15 MG CHOL, 722 MG SOD, 8 G PRO, 43 G CAR, 6 G FIBER

Make ahead » To freeze, omit the toasts and the scallions. Let the soup cool, transfer to freezer-safe containers and freeze for up to 3 months.

Barbecue glazed pork with green rice

ACTIVE 25 MIN • **TOTAL** 25 MIN • **SERVES** 4 • **COST PER SERVING** $1.70

½ cup long-grain white rice

1 cup frozen edamame, thawed

2 scallions, thinly sliced

4 oz snap peas, thinly sliced
   crosswise

2 Tbsp ketchup

2 Tbsp low-sodium soy sauce

2 Tbsp packed light brown sugar

1 Tbsp finely grated fresh ginger

½ tsp chili powder

1 Tbsp olive oil

   Kosher salt and pepper

1 1¼-lb pork tenderloin

   Toasted sesame seeds,
   for serving

❶ Heat oven to 400°F. Cook the rice according to package directions. Fluff with a fork and fold in the edamame and scallions, then the snap peas.

❷ Meanwhile, in a small bowl, combine the ketchup, soy sauce, sugar, ginger and chili powder. Heat the oil in a large oven-safe skillet over medium-high heat. Season the pork with ½ tsp pepper and cook, turning occasionally, until browned on all sides, 4 to 5 minutes total.

❸ Brush the pork with half the ketchup mixture and roast until the internal temperature reaches 145°F, 12 to 15 minutes.

❹ Transfer the pork to a cutting board, brush with the remaining ketchup mixture and let rest for 5 minutes before slicing. Serve with the rice and sprinkle with the sesame seeds, if desired.

♥ **PER SERVING** 378 CAL, 9 G FAT (2 G SAT FAT), 83 MG CHOL, 430 MG SOD, 36 G PRO, 36 G CAR, 3 G FIBER

Cook's tip » This recipe is perfect for outdoor grilling. Grill the pork (without the glaze) over medium-high heat, turning occasionally, until the internal temperature reaches 140°F, about 15 minutes. Continue cooking, brushing with the glaze and turning occasionally, until the pork registers 145°F, 3 to 5 minutes more. Transfer to a cutting board, brush with any remaining glaze and let rest for 5 minutes before slicing.

Chickpea and red pepper soup with quinoa

ACTIVE 25 MIN • **TOTAL** 25 MIN • **SERVES** 4 • **COST PER SERVING** $2.91

½ cup quinoa

2 Tbsp olive oil

1 medium onion, chopped

1 carrot, chopped

2 stalks celery, chopped

3 cloves garlic, finely chopped

1 Tbsp smoked paprika

Kosher salt and pepper

1 yellow pepper, cut into
½-in. pieces

1 red pepper, cut into
½-in pieces

2 15-oz cans low-sodium
chickpeas, rinsed

2 cups low-sodium vegetable
broth

2 Tbsp red wine vinegar

Chopped fresh parsley,
for serving

❶ Cook the quinoa according to package directions.

❷ Meanwhile, heat the oil in a Dutch oven or large heavy-bottomed pot. Add the onion, carrot and celery and cook, covered, stirring occasionally, for 6 minutes.

❸ Add the garlic, paprika and ¼ tsp each salt and pepper and cook, stirring, for 1 minute. Add the peppers and cook, stirring occasionally, for 5 minutes.

❹ Add the chickpeas, broth and 1 cup water and bring to a boil. Reduce heat and simmer until the vegetables are tender, 5 to 8 minutes. Stir in the vinegar and cooked quinoa. Serve topped with parsley, if desired.

♥ **PER SERVING** 412 CAL, 10 G FAT (1 G SAT FAT), 0 MG CHOL, 281 MG SOD, 16 G PRO, 65 G CAR, 13 G FIBER

Make ahead » Prepare the soup (without the vinegar and quinoa) and refrigerate for up to 1 week. When ready to serve, prepare the quinoa and reheat the soup in a medium pot over medium heat. Stir in the vinegar and cooked quinoa just before serving.

Chicken cutlets with apple and celery slaw

ACTIVE 30 MIN • **TOTAL** 30 MIN • **SERVES** 4
COST PER SERVING $1.41

4	6-oz boneless, skinless chicken breasts
	Kosher salt and pepper
¾	cup panko bread crumbs
3	Tbsp olive oil
¼	cup lowfat sour cream
1	tsp Dijon mustard
1	Tbsp fresh lemon juice
2	stalks celery, thinly sliced on a diagonal
1	Granny Smith apple, cut into matchsticks
1	Tbsp chopped chives

❶ Slice the chicken breasts in half horizontally to create 8 small chicken cutlets; season with ½ tsp salt and ¼ tsp pepper and coat in the bread crumbs, pressing gently to help them adhere.

❷ Heat 2 Tbsp oil in a large skillet over medium-high heat. In two batches, cook the chicken until golden brown and cooked through, 2 to 3 minutes per side, adding more oil to the skillet if necessary. Transfer the chicken to plates.

❸ Meanwhile, in a large bowl, whisk together the sour cream, mustard, lemon juice, remaining Tbsp oil and ¼ tsp each salt and pepper. Add the celery and apple and toss to combine; fold in the chives. Serve with the chicken.

PER SERVING 373 CAL, 14 G FAT (3 G SAT FAT), 96 MG CHOL, 550 MG SOD, 37 G PRO, 24 G CAR, 2 G FIBER

Switch it up » Try the apple-celery slaw with seared pork chops or piled on a turkey sandwich.

Roasted acorn squash salad

ACTIVE 25 MIN • **TOTAL** 45 MIN • **SERVES** 4
COST PER SERVING $3.05

¼ tsp crushed red pepper flakes

¼ tsp ground cinnamon

Kosher salt

1 large acorn squash (about 2 lb), seeded and sliced ½ in. thick

3 Tbsp olive oil

1 cup apple cider

2 cups pearl couscous

3 Tbsp red wine vinegar

2 tsp Dijon mustard

½ small red onion, thinly sliced

4 cups baby spinach

Roughly chopped toasted pecans, for serving

> *Easy upgrade »* For a decadent twist, sprinkle ¼ cup dried cherries and crumbled blue cheese over the salad before serving.

❶ Heat oven to 425°F. In a small bowl, combine the red pepper, cinnamon and ½ tsp salt. On a large rimmed baking sheet, toss the squash with 2 Tbsp oil, then the spice mixture. Arrange the squash in an even layer and roast, turning once, until lightly golden brown and tender, 18 to 22 minutes.

❷ Meanwhile, bring the cider to a boil in a small saucepan. Reduce heat and simmer until liquid has reduced to ¼ cup, about 15 minutes. Cook the couscous according to package directions.

❸ In a large bowl, whisk together the reduced cider, vinegar, mustard and the remaining 1 Tbsp oil.

❹ Add the cooked couscous, onion and spinach to the dressing. Toss until the spinach is beginning to wilt, then carefully fold in the squash. Sprinkle with the pecans, if desired.

♥ **PER SERVING** 488 CAL, 10.5 G FAT (1.5 G SAT FAT), 0 MG CHOL, 353 MG SOD, 10 G PRO, 88 G CAR, 11 G FIBER

Grilled chicken and peaches

ACTIVE 15 MIN • **TOTAL** 30 MIN • **SERVES** 4 • **COST PER SERVING** $2.27

- 1 Tbsp white wine vinegar
- ½ tsp grated ginger
- 3 Tbsp plus 1 tsp olive oil
  Kosher salt and pepper
- 2 medium red onions, sliced into ½-in.-thick rounds
- 4 6-oz boneless, skinless chicken breasts
- 3 peaches, cut into wedges
- 1 bunch spinach, thick stems removed (about 4 cups)

❶ Heat grill to medium-high. In a small bowl, whisk together the vinegar, ginger, 1 Tbsp olive oil and ⅛ tsp each salt and pepper; set aside.

❷ Brush the onions with 1 Tbsp oil and season with ¼ tsp each salt and pepper. Brush the chicken with 1 tsp oil, and season with ½ tsp each salt and pepper. In a bowl, toss the peaches with the remaining Tbsp oil.

❸ Grill the chicken and onions until the chicken is cooked through and the onions are tender, 5 to 6 minutes per side. Grill the peaches (reserve the bowl) until charred, 2 minutes per side.

❹ Transfer the peaches and onions to the bowl. Add the spinach and vinaigrette and toss to combine. Serve with the chicken.

♥ **PER SERVING** 326 CAL, 12 G FAT (2 G SAT FAT), 94 MG CHOL, 529 MG SOD, 37 G PRO, 17 G CAR, 12 G SUGAR, 3 G FIBER

> *Switch it up »* Turn this salad into a sandwich by slicing the chicken, then layering it with the peaches, onions and spinach between two slices of bread. Or wrap it all up in a tortilla or stuff into a pita.

Vegetable lasagna

ACTIVE 40 MIN • **TOTAL** 1 HR 15 MIN • **SERVES** 6 • **COST PER SERVING** $1.52

1   Tbsp olive oil

1   medium onion, finely chopped

Kosher salt and pepper

2   cloves garlic, finely chopped

½   cup fresh flat-leaf parsley, chopped

1   16-oz container low-sodium 1% cottage cheese

1   10-oz pkg frozen broccoli florets, thawed, chopped and squeezed of excess moisture

2   Tbsp grated Parmesan

2   tsp grated lemon zest

3   oz part-skim mozzarella, coarsely grated (about ¾ cup)

2   cups baby spinach, chopped

1   cup fresh basil, chopped (optional)

2   cups low-sodium marinara sauce

6   no-boil lasagna noodles

❶ Heat oven to 425°F. Heat the oil in a medium skillet over medium heat. Add the onion, ¼ tsp each salt and pepper and cook, covered, stirring occasionally, until very tender, 8 to 10 minutes. Add the garlic and cook for 1 minute; stir in the parsley.

❷ Meanwhile, in a food processor, purée the cottage cheese and broccoli until smooth; transfer to a bowl. Mix in the onion mixture, Parmesan, lemon zest, ½ cup mozzarella and ¼ tsp each salt and pepper, then fold in the spinach and basil (if using).

❸ Spread ½ cup marinara on the bottom of an 8-in. square baking dish. Top with 2 noodles and spread one-third of the remaining marinara (about ½ cup) over the top. Dollop with half the broccoli mixture.

❹ Top with 2 noodles, half of the remaining marinara and then the remaining broccoli mixture. Top with the remaining noodles and marinara, then sprinkle with the remaining ¼ cup mozzarella.

❺ Cover tightly with nonstick foil and bake for 20 minutes. Uncover and bake until the noodles are tender and the top is golden brown, 12 to 15 minutes. Let rest for 5 minutes before slicing.

♥ **PER SERVING** 252 CAL, 7.5 G FAT (2.5 G SAT FAT), 12 MG CHOL, 382 MG SOD, 18 G PRO, 27 G CAR, 3 G FIBER

Make ahead » Line the baking dish with foil, leaving a 3-in. overhang on two sides. Prepare the lasagna as directed. After baking, allow it to cool in the dish. Use the overhangs to lift it out; wrap tightly in plastic, then foil, and freeze for up to 2 months. To serve: Let thaw in the refrigerator, remove the foil and plastic, and transfer the lasagna to a casserole dish. Reheat in a 375°F oven, about 20 minutes.

Sweet and spicy chicken stir fry

ACTIVE 25 MIN • **TOTAL** 40 MIN • **SERVES** 4
COST PER SERVING $1.72

- 1 cup brown rice
- ½ cup apricot preserves
- 2 Tbsp cider vinegar
- 1 Tbsp grated fresh ginger
- ¼ to ½ tsp crushed red pepper flakes
- 3 tsp canola oil
- 1 lb boneless, skinless chicken breasts, sliced crosswise ¼-in. thick
- 2 medium carrots, cut into very thin strips
- ½ lb snow peas, halved diagonally lengthwise

❶ Cook the rice according to package directions.

❷ Meanwhile, in a small bowl, combine the apricot preserves, vinegar, ginger, red pepper flakes and 1 Tbsp water; set aside.

❸ Heat 2 tsp oil in a large skillet over medium-high heat. In batches, cook the chicken until golden brown, 1 to 2 minutes per side; transfer to a plate.

❹ Add the carrots, snow peas and remaining tsp oil and cook, tossing, for 2 minutes. Return the chicken to the skillet, add the apricot mixture, and cook until the chicken is cooked through and the vegetables are just tender, 2 to 3 minutes more. Serve over the rice.

♥ **PER SERVING** 458 CAL, 7 G FAT (1 G SAT FAT), 72 MG CHOL, 179 MG SOD, 30 G PRO, 69 G CAR, 5 G FIBER

> ***Switch it up »*** This apricot sauce is terrific paired with pork or salmon. Trim pork tenderloin and cut into ¼-in.-thick pieces or cut skinless salmon fillet into large chunks. Cook the pork like the chicken. If using salmon, cook until opaque throughout, about 2 minutes per side. Gently toss the salmon with the vegetable mixture just before serving.

Steak with chickpea, pomegranate and arugula salad

ACTIVE 25 MIN • **TOTAL** 25 MIN • **SERVES** 4
COST PER SERVING $4.14

2	Tbsp plus 1 tsp olive oil
1	lb strip steak (1 in. thick)
	Kosher salt and pepper
1	15-oz can chickpeas, rinsed
½	cup pomegranate seeds (from 1 small pomegranate)
¼	cup fresh mint, chopped
2	scallions, sliced
1	Tbsp fresh lemon juice
4	cups baby arugula

❶ Heat 1 tsp oil in a large skillet over medium-high heat. Season the steak with ½ tsp salt and ¼ tsp pepper and cook to desired doneness, 5 to 6 minutes per side for medium-rare. Let rest for at least 5 minutes before slicing.

❷ Meanwhile, in a large bowl, combine the chickpeas, pomegranate seeds, mint, scallions, lemon juice, remaining 2 Tbsp oil, and ¼ tsp each salt and pepper. Fold in the arugula. Serve with the steak.

PER SERVING 394 CAL, 23 G FAT (6 G SAT FAT), 69 MG CHOL, 598 MG SOD, 27 G PRO, 21 G CAR, 6 G FIBER

Prep tip » To easlily remove the seeds from a pomegranate, cut ½ in. from the top, then score the skin along each section. Submerge the pomegranate in a bowl of water and gently pull apart the sections. Still working underwater, remove the white membranes and pull apart the seeds. The seeds will sink to the bottom of the bowl and the membranes will float. Discard the skin, membrane and water leaving the seeds behind.

Slow cooker chicken and barley stew

ACTIVE 15 MIN • **TOTAL** 4 HR 15 MIN OR 6 HR 15 MIN • **SERVES** 4 • **COST PER SERVING** $1.29

2 medium carrots, cut into 1-in. pieces

2 stalks celery, sliced

1 medium onion, chopped

½ cup barley

½ cup dried navy beans

1 14.5-oz can low-sodium chicken broth

6 sprigs fresh thyme, plus leaves for serving

Kosher salt and pepper

1½ lb chicken legs (2 to 3), skin removed

❶ In a 5- to 6-qt slow cooker, combine the carrots, celery, onion, barley, beans, broth, thyme, 2 cups water, ½ tsp salt and ¼ tsp pepper.

❷ Nestle the chicken legs into the vegetable mixture and cook, covered, until the chicken is cooked through and shreds easily and the barley and beans are tender, 5 to 6 hours on low or 3 to 4 hours on high.

❸ Remove and discard the chicken bones, any large pieces of cartilage and thyme. Using a fork, break the chicken into large pieces. Spoon into bowls and top with additional pepper and thyme, if desired.

♥ **PER SERVING** 321 CAL, 5.5 G FAT (1.5 G SAT FAT), 90 MG CHOL, 431 MG SOD, 28 G PRO, 40 G CAR, 12 G FIBER

Prep tip » To easily remove raw chicken skin, use a paper towel to grip the skin and pull it down and off the drumstick.

Lemon chili chicken

ACTIVE 15 MIN • **TOTAL** 30 MIN • **SERVES** 4 • **COST PER SERVING** $1.52

1 cup long-grain white rice

4 scallions, thinly sliced, plus more for serving

2 red chilies or jalapeños, (seeded for less heat, if desired), thinly sliced

1 lemon, thinly sliced

4 6-oz boneless, skinless chicken breasts

1 Tbsp Dijon mustard
 Kosher salt and pepper

2 Tbsp olive oil

1 lb asparagus

1 Heat the oven to 425°F. Cook the rice according to package directions. Tear off four 12-in. squares of parchment paper.

2 Divide the scallions, peppers and lemon among the squares. Brush the chicken with the mustard and season with ½ tsp each salt and pepper; place on top of the lemon and scallions.

3 Drizzle the chicken with 1 Tbsp oil. Bring the parchment ends together and twist to seal and form loose packets. Place on a baking sheet and roast until the chicken is cooked through, 15 minutes.

4 Meanwhile, on a large rimmed baking sheet, toss the asparagus with the remaining Tbsp oil and season with ¼ tsp each salt and pepper. Roast (on the rack below the chicken) until golden brown and tender, 10 to 12 minutes.

5 Carefully open the packets (hot steam will escape). Serve the chicken and vegetables with the asparagus and rice. Sprinkle with additional scallions, if desired.

PER SERVING 293 CAL, 11.5 G FAT (2 G SAT FAT), 109 MG CHOL, 667 MG SOD, 39 G PRO, 8 G CAR, 3 G FIBER

Prep tip » Take this tasty dinner outside to the grill. Make the packets using foil instead of parchment and cook the packets, covered, over medium-high heat, shaking occasionally. After 5 minutes, add the asparagus to the grill and cook, turning occasionally, until the asparagus are lightly charred and tender and the chicken is cooked through.

Blackened salmon with pineapple rice

ACTIVE 25 MIN • **TOTAL** 25 MIN • **SERVES** 4
COST PER SERVING $3.16

1	cup long-grain white rice
8	oz fresh pineapple, cut into ½-in. pieces
1	to 2 jalapeños, seeded and finely chopped
½	cup fresh cilantro, chopped
1¼	lb skinless salmon fillet, cut into 4 pieces
2	Tbsp blackening or Cajun seasoning (no salt added)

❶ Cook the rice according to package directions. Fluff with a fork and fold in the pineapple, jalapeños and cilantro.

❷ Meanwhile, heat a large skillet over medium heat. Coat both sides of the salmon with the seasoning and cook, covered, until opaque throughout and blackened, 3 to 4 minutes per side. Serve with the rice.

♥ PER SERVING 455 CAL, 11 G FAT (2 G SAT FAT), 90 MG CHOL, 75 MG SOD, 37 G PRO, 50 G CAR, 2 G FIBER

Love your leftovers » Use leftover salmon for fish tacos. Flake the cooked salmon and pile in flour tortillas with finely chopped pineapple, fresh cilantro, tomato salsa and a drizzle of sour cream.

Chicken enchilada bake

ACTIVE 20 MIN • **TOTAL** 35 MIN • **SERVES** 6 • **COST PER SERVING** $1.66

Kosher salt and pepper

1 lb boneless, skinless chicken breasts

3 Tbsp olive oil

1 large onion, chopped

2 cloves garlic, finely chopped

1 poblano or green bell pepper, thinly sliced

2 bell peppers (orange and yellow), thinly sliced

1 cup frozen corn kernels

½ cup lowfat sour cream

2 Tbsp fresh lime juice

1 cup fresh cilantro, chopped

4 oz Pepper Jack cheese, coarsely grated (1 cup)

8 9 x 14-in. sheets fillo, thawed

Chili powder, for dusting

Cook's tip » Also known as filo and phyllo, this paper-thin dough contains no butter and has a distinctively light, crisp texture. It dries out quickly, so keep the dough covered with plastic wrap and a damp towel while you work. Wrap leftover fillo tightly in plastic wrap; refrigerate for up to 2 weeks or freeze for up to 8 months.

❶ Heat oven to 425°F. Fill a medium saucepan halfway with water. Bring to a boil; add 1 tsp salt. Add the chicken, reduce heat and simmer until cooked through, 10 to 12 minutes. Transfer to a plate and let cool; shred.

❷ Meanwhile, heat 2 Tbsp oil in a large skillet over medium heat. Add the onion and ¼ tsp each salt and pepper and cook, covered, stirring occasionally, for 5 minutes. Add the garlic and peppers and cook, covered, stirring occasionally, until just tender, 5 to 6 minutes. Stir in the corn, sour cream and lime juice. Fold in the chicken, cilantro and cheese. Transfer to a 2-qt casserole dish.

❸ Working on a piece of parchment paper, brush one sheet of fillo with some of the remaining oil and sprinkle with chili powder, if desired (keep the other sheets covered with plastic wrap and a damp cloth so they don't dry out). Scrunch the sheet together and place on top of the chicken mixture. Repeat with the remaining fillo sheets. Bake until golden brown, 12 to 15 minutes.

PER SERVING 375 CAL, 18 G FAT (6 G SAT FAT), 68 MG CHOL, 475 MG SOD, 25 G PRO, 29 G CAR, 2 G FIBER

Sweet and spicy pork with black bean salad

ACTIVE 15 MIN • **TOTAL** 30 MIN • **SERVES** 4 • **COST PER SERVING** $2.82

1 Tbsp brown sugar

2 tsp ancho or regular chili powder

1 tsp ground cumin

2 Tbsp olive oil

Kosher salt and pepper

1 1¼-lb pork tenderloin

1 15-oz can black beans, rinsed

1 pint grape tomatoes, halved

3 scallions, thinly sliced

1 jalapeño (seeded for less heat), finely chopped

1 Tbsp red wine vinegar

½ cup fresh cilantro, chopped

❶ Heat oven to 425°F. Line a baking sheet with foil or parchment paper. In a small bowl, combine the sugar, chili powder, cumin, 1 Tbsp oil, ½ tsp salt and ¼ tsp pepper.

❷ Rub the spice mixture all over the pork, place on the prepared baking sheet, and roast until the pork registers 145°F, 18 to 22 minutes. Let rest for at least 5 minutes before slicing.

❸ Meanwhile, in a large bowl, toss together the beans, tomatoes, scallions, jalapeño, vinegar, remaining Tbsp oil, ½ tsp salt and ¼ tsp pepper; fold in the cilantro. Serve with the pork.

....

♥ **PER SERVING** 344 CAL, 11 G FAT (2 G SAT FAT), 78 MG CHOL, 796 MG SOD, 35 G PRO, 25 G CAR, 9 G FIBER

Cook's tip » Spice-rubbed pork is perfect for grilling. Grill over medium-high heat, turning occasionally, to 145°F, 18 to 22 minutes.

Quick chicken curry with tomatoes and peas

ACTIVE 25 MIN • **TOTAL** 25 MIN • **SERVES** 4 • **COST PER SERVING** $2.14

1	cup long-grain white rice
2	Tbsp olive oil
1½	lb boneless, skinless chicken breasts, cut into 2-in. pieces
2	tsp curry powder
	Kosher salt and pepper
¾	cup dry white wine
1	onion, sliced ¼ in. thick
2	cloves garlic, finely chopped
1	Tbsp grated fresh ginger
1	pint grape tomatoes, halved
¾	cup frozen peas, thawed

1 Cook the rice according to package directions. Meanwhile, heat 1 Tbsp oil in a large skillet over medium-high heat. Season the chicken with the curry powder and ¼ tsp each salt and pepper and cook until browned, 2 to 3 minutes per side. Transfer to a bowl. Add the wine to the skillet and cook, scraping up any brown bits, for 2 minutes. Transfer to the bowl with the chicken.

2 Wipe out the skillet and heat the remaining Tbsp oil over medium heat. Add the onion and cook, covered, stirring occasionally, for 6 minutes. Stir in the garlic and ginger and cook for 1 minute.

3 Return the chicken and wine to the skillet, add the tomatoes and peas, and cook until heated through, about 3 minutes. Serve over the rice.

PER SERVING 398 CAL, 9 G FAT (7 G SAT FAT), 98 MG CHOL, 267 MG SOD, 42 G PRO, 46 G CAR, 3 G FIBER

Switch it up » Turn this into a one-pot meal by omitting the rice and making couscous instead. Place 1 cup couscous in a large bowl, add 1 cup warm water, cover and let sit until all the water is absorbed, about 15 minutes. Fluff with a fork before serving.

Tex-Mex black bean soup

ACTIVE 15 MIN • **TOTAL** 20 MIN • **SERVES** 4
COST PER SERVING $2.13

1	Tbsp olive oil
1	medium onion, chopped
1	green bell pepper, cut into ¼-in. pieces
	Kosher salt and pepper
1	Tbsp chopped chipotle in adobo sauce
1	15-oz can low-sodium black beans, rinsed
1	15-oz can refried black beans
2	cups low-sodium vegetable broth
1	avocado, diced
½	cup refrigerated fresh salsa
¼	cup lowfat sour cream
	Fresh cilantro, for serving

1 Heat the oil in a large pot or Dutch oven over medium heat. Add the onion and green pepper, season with ¼ tsp each salt and pepper and cook, covered, stirring occasionally, for 5 minutes. Stir in the chipotle and adobo.

2 Stir in the beans, refried beans and broth and bring to a boil. Reduce heat and simmer for 2 minutes.

3 Divide the soup among 4 bowls and top with the avocado, salsa, sour cream and cilantro, if desired.

....

PER SERVING 309 CAL, 12 G FAT (2 G SAT FAT), 2.5 MG CHOL, 819 MG SOD, 12 G PRO, 43 G CAR, 16 G FIBER

Make ahead » Freeze the soup (without the toppings) for up to 3 months. Thaw in the refrigerator overnight, then reheat in a medium saucepan over medium heat.

Ravioli with apples, bacon and spinach

ACTIVE 20 MIN • **TOTAL** 20 MIN • **SERVES** 4
COST PER SERVING $1.71

16	oz fresh or frozen cheese ravioli
6	slices bacon
2	Tbsp olive oil
2	cloves garlic, thinly sliced
1	crisp red apple (Braeburn or Gala), quartered and thinly sliced
1	bunch fresh spinach, thick stems discarded
	Kosher salt and pepper
1	Tbsp fresh lemon juice

❶ Cook the ravioli according to package directions.

❷ Meanwhile, cook the bacon in a skillet over medium heat until crisp, 6 to 8 minutes. Transfer to a paper towel–lined plate; break into pieces when cool.

❸ Wipe out the skillet; heat the oil over medium heat. Add the garlic; cook, stirring occasionally, until golden brown, 1 to 2 minutes. Add the apple; cook, tossing, for 1 minute.

❹ Add the spinach, ½ tsp salt and ¼ tsp pepper; cook, tossing, until beginning to wilt, 1 to 2 minutes. Fold in the lemon juice and bacon. Serve over the ravioli.

PER SERVING 385 CAL, 18 G FAT (6G SAT FAT), 38 MG CHOL, 823 SOD, 41G CAR, 7G PRO, 4G FIBER

Switch it up » Cut the calories and fat in this recipe by using potato and onion pierogies instead of cheese ravioli.

Cod cakes with orange and radish salad

ACTIVE 20 MIN • **TOTAL** 30 MIN • **SERVES** 4 • **COST PER SERVING** $4.62

2   navel oranges

1½   lb cod fillet, cut into 2-in. pieces

2   scallions, thinly sliced

1   large egg white

    Kosher salt and pepper

1   cup panko bread crumbs

3   Tbsp olive oil

1   bunch radishes, thinly sliced

1   jalapeño, thinly sliced

½   sweet onion, thinly sliced

❶ Heat oven to 400°F. Grate 2 tsp orange zest and place in a food processor. Add the cod, scallions, egg white, ½ tsp salt and ¼ tsp pepper, and pulse until combined and coarsely chopped (do not purée).

❷ Form the cod mixture into eight ¾-in.-thick patties. Coat each patty in the bread crumbs, pressing gently to help them adhere.

❸ Heat 1 Tbsp oil in a large skillet over medium-high heat. Add 4 cakes and cook until golden brown, 2 to 3 minutes per side; transfer to a baking sheet. Wipe out the skillet and repeat with 1 Tbsp oil and the remaining cod cakes. Transfer the cod cakes to the oven and bake until cooked through, 5 to 8 minutes.

❹ Meanwhile, cut away the peel and white pith of the oranges and thinly slice into rounds. In a medium bowl, gently toss the oranges, radishes, jalapeño, onion, the remaining Tbsp oil and ¼ tsp each salt and pepper. Serve with the cod cakes.

♥ **PER SERVING** 357 CAL, 10 G FAT (1 G SAT FAT), 65 MG CHOL, 539 MG SOD, 31 G PRO, 34 G CAR, 3 G FIBER

Make ahead » The uncooked cakes can be shaped (but not coated in the bread crumbs), placed in a single layer on a plate, covered and refrigerated for up to 2 days or frozen for up to 2 months. Before cooking, thaw the cakes if frozen and coat in the bread crumbs.

Steak salad with arugula and grapefruit

ACTIVE 20 MIN • **TOTAL** 20 MIN • **SERVES** 4 • **COST PER SERVING** $3.12

1   lb sirloin steak, trimmed of excess fat

Kosher salt and pepper

2   red or pink grapefruits

2   Tbsp fresh lime juice

2   Tbsp olive oil

1   small avocado

6   cups baby arugula

2   cups fresh cilantro

Unsalted roasted pepitas (hulled pumpkin seeds), for serving

① Heat broiler. Line a broiler-proof rimmed baking sheet with foil. Place the steak on the prepared pan and season with ¼ tsp each salt and pepper. Broil to desired doneness, 4 to 5 minutes per side for medium-rare. Transfer to a cutting board and let rest for at least 5 minutes before slicing.

② Meanwhile, cut away the peel and white pith from the grapefruits. Cut the grapefruits into segments. In a small bowl, whisk together the lime juice, olive oil and ¼ tsp each salt and pepper.

③ Dice the avocado. In a large bowl, gently toss the arugula, cilantro, avocado, grapefruit and sliced steak. Drizzle with the lime juice mixture and sprinkle with pepitas, if desired.

♥ **PER SERVING** 298 CAL, 16 G FAT (3 G SAT FAT), 60 MG CHOL, 783 MG SOD, 24 G PRO, 16 G CAR, 4 G FIBER

Love your leftovers » Make a fresh take on a steak sandwich: Layer leftover sliced steak, arugula, grapefruit and avocado on ciabatta bread or baguette and drizzle with the lime juice mixture.

Orange chicken with peppers and onions

ACTIVE 20 MIN • **TOTAL** 20 MIN • **SERVES** 4
COST PER SERVING $3.00

1	cup long-grain white rice
2	Tbsp olive oil
4	6-oz boneless, skinless chicken breast, cut in thirds
	Kosher salt and black pepper
1	onion, sliced
1	red pepper, sliced
2	cloves garlic, chopped
2	oranges, juiced (about ½ cup)
½	cup pitted Kalamata olives, halved

❶ Cook the rice according to package directions.

❷ Meanwhile, heat 1 Tbsp oil in a medium skillet over medium-high heat. Season the chicken with ½ tsp salt and ¼ tsp of pepper and cook until golden brown, 2 to 3 minutes per side; transfer to a plate.

❸ Add the onion, red pepper, garlic and remaining 1 Tbsp oil to the skillet; season with ¼ tsp each salt and pepper. Cook, stirring occasionally, until just tender, 3 to 4 minutes.

❹ Nestle the chicken among the vegetables. Add the orange juice and olives, and simmer until the vegetables are tender and the chicken is cooked through, 3 to 4 minutes more. Serve with the rice.

PER SERVING 447 CAL, 14 G FAT (1.5 G SAT FAT), 107 MG CHOL, 905 MG SOD, 41 G PRO, 51 G CAR, 2 G FIBER

Love your leftovers » Slice leftover chicken and stuff it in pita bread or wrap in a large tortilla with the vegetables and baby arugula or spinach.

Meatless-but-you'd-never-know-it chili

ACTIVE 10 MIN • **TOTAL** 5 HR 10 MIN OR 8 HR 10 MIN • **SERVES** 8
COST PER SERVING $1.38

¾ cup wheat berries, soaked overnight

2 large carrots, coarsely grated

1 medium red onion, coarsely chopped

1 large clove garlic, finely chopped

1 28-oz can crushed tomatoes

1 28-oz can tomato purée

2 tsp dried oregano

2 tsp ground cumin

½ tsp cayenne pepper

   Kosher salt

2 15-oz cans kidney, pinto or black beans, rinsed

1 16-oz pkg frozen corn kernels

1 pepper (red or green), cut into ¼-in. pieces

1 tsp jalapeño hot sauce, plus more for serving

   Sour cream, grated Cheddar and tortilla chips, for serving

Make ahead » Freeze the chili for up to 3 months. Thaw in the fridge overnight and reheat in a medium saucepan, covered, adding ½ cup water if it seems too thick.

❶ Rinse and drain the wheat berries and place them in a 5- to 6-qt slow cooker. Add the carrots, onion, garlic, tomatoes, tomato purée, oregano, cumin, cayenne and ½ tsp salt; mix to combine. Cover and cook on low for 6 to 8 hours or on high for 4 to 5 hours.

❷ Stir in the beans, corn, pepper and hot sauce and cook until heated through, about 5 minutes. Serve with the sour cream, Cheddar, tortilla chips and additional hot sauce, if desired.

♥ **PER SERVING** 360 CAL, 2 G FAT (0 G SAT FAT), 0 MG CHOL, 744 MG SOD, 18 G PRO, 72 G CAR, 18 G FIBER

Roast beef lettuce wraps

ACTIVE 15 MIN • **TOTAL** 15 MIN • **SERVES** 4 • **COST PER SERVING** $3.33

¼ cup rice vinegar

1 Tbsp honey

Kosher salt and pepper

1 large shallot, finely chopped

1 Tbsp finely grated ginger

1 head Boston or Bibb lettuce, leaves separated

¾ lb thinly sliced roast beef, torn into 2-in. pieces

2 plums, thinly sliced

1 small seedless cucumber, halved lengthwise and thinly sliced

1 large carrot, cut into matchsticks

½ cup fresh mint leaves

❶ In a small bowl, whisk together the vinegar, honey, ½ tsp salt and ¼ tsp pepper; stir in the shallot and ginger.

❷ Fill the lettuce leaves with the roast beef, plums, cucumber, carrot and mint. Serve with the vinaigrette for drizzling.

PER SERVING 160 CAL, 3 G FAT (2 G SAT FAT), 38 MG CHOL, 966 MG SOD, 19 G PRO, 18 G CAR, 3 G FIBER

Switch it up » Instead of lettuce wraps, make a cold noodle salad: Place one 8-oz package rice noodles in a large bowl, cover with warm tap water and let them soak until soft, about 30 minutes. Drain and toss with all the ingredients except the lettuce.

Fettuccine "Alfredo"

ACTIVE 35 MIN • **TOTAL** 35 MIN • **SERVES** 4 • **COST PER SERVING** 80¢

½ head cauliflower (about 1 lb), chopped

12 oz fettuccine

2 Tbsp olive oil

1 large onion, finely chopped

Kosher salt and pepper

2 cloves garlic, finely chopped

1 Tbsp all-purpose flour

1 cup 1% milk

¼ cup grated Romano cheese

Pinch cayenne pepper

Chopped fresh flat-leaf parsley, for serving

1 Place the cauliflower and 2½ cups water in a pot and simmer until the cauliflower falls apart when squeezed, 15 to 18 minutes. Transfer the cauliflower and any remaining liquid in the pot to a blender and purée until smooth (add extra water, if necessary).

2 Meanwhile, cook the pasta according to package directions (omit salt). Reserve 1 cup of the cooking liquid, drain the pasta and return it to the pot.

3 Heat the oil in a medium skillet over medium heat. Add the onion, ½ tsp each salt and pepper and cook, covered, stirring occasionally, until very tender, 8 to 10 minutes.

4 Add the garlic and cook for 1 minute. Sprinkle with the flour and cook, stirring, for 1 minute more. Stir in the milk and simmer until slightly thickened, about 3 minutes. Stir in the Romano.

5 Add the milk mixture and cayenne to the blender; purée until smooth. Toss the cauliflower mixture with the pasta, adding some of the reserved cooking liquid if the mixture seems dry. Top with pepper and parsley before serving, if desired.

♥ **PER** SERVING 466 CAL, 10.5 G FAT (2.5 G SAT FAT), 7 MG CHOL, 366 MG SOD, 18 G PRO, 77 G CAR, 6 G FIBER

Make ahead » The "Alfredo" sauce can be prepared and refrigerated for up to 5 days. When ready to serve, warm in a medium saucepan over medium heat, whisking occasionally, until heated through.

Shrimp tacos with citrus slaw

ACTIVE 20 MIN • **TOTAL** 20 MIN • **SERVES** 4
COST PER SERVING $4.17

¼	small green cabbage, thinly sliced
1	red pepper, thinly sliced
½	small white onion, thinly sliced
¼	cup fresh lime juice (from 2 to 3 limes)
2	Tbsp plus 1 tsp olive oil
	Kosher salt and pepper
1½	lb large shrimp, peeled and deveined, tails removed
½	tsp ground chipotle chiles or chili powder
8	small flour tortillas, warmed

1 In a large bowl, combine the cabbage, red pepper, onion, lime juice, 2 Tbsp oil, ¼ tsp salt and ½ tsp pepper. Let sit, tossing occasionally, for at least 5 minutes.

2 Heat the remaining tsp oil in a large nonstick skillet over medium-high heat. Season the shrimp with the chipotle chiles and ½ tsp salt; cook until opaque throughout, 2 to 3 minutes per side.

3 Spoon the shrimp into the tortillas and top with the citrus slaw.

PER SERVING 339 CAL, 9 G FAT (2 G SAT FAT), 252 MG CHOL, 578 MG SOD, 32 G PRO, 31 G CAR, 13 G FIBER

Switch it up » Instead of shrimp, try these tacos with seared white fish, salmon or boneless skinless chicken breast. Cook 6-oz pieces of fish, then flake before filling the tortillas or cut the chicken into strips and sauté until golden brown and cooked through.

White fish with chickpea ragu

ACTIVE 15 MIN • **TOTAL** 25 MIN • **SERVES** 4
COST PER SERVING $3.46

1	Tbsp olive oil
1	onion, chopped
2	cloves garlic, finely chopped
	Kosher salt and pepper
½	tsp paprika (preferably smoked)
1	15-oz can chickpeas, rinsed
1	14.5-oz can diced tomatoes
1	1¼-lb piece cod or halibut fillet (1 in. thick), cut into 4 pieces
½	cup fresh flat-leaf parsley, chopped

❶ Heat the oil in a large skillet over medium heat. Add the onion, garlic and ¼ tsp each salt and pepper and cook, stirring, until beginning to soften, 5 to 6 minutes. Stir in the paprika and cook for 1 minute.

❷ Add the chickpeas and tomatoes and bring to a boil. Reduce heat and simmer, stirring occasionally, for 4 minutes.

❸ Season the fish with ¼ tsp each salt and pepper and nestle it among the chickpeas. Simmer, covered, until the fish is opaque throughout and the sauce has thickened, 8 to 10 minutes. Stir in the parsley before serving.

♥ **PER SERVING** 285 CAL, 6 G FAT (1 G SAT FAT), 61 MG CHOL, 743 MG SOD, 32 G PRO, 25 G CAR, 6 G FIBER,

***Switch it up* »** Try tossing the chickpea ragu with whole-grain penne or other short pasta.

Sautéed chicken cutlets and cherry tomatoes with spinach orzo

ACTIVE 25 MIN • **TOTAL** 25 MIN • **SERVES** 4 • **COST PER SERVING** $1.73

¾ cup orzo

1 bunch spinach, thick stems discarded, leaves torn

Kosher salt and pepper

2 Tbsp olive oil

8 small chicken cutlets (about 1½ lb total)

1 pint grape tomatoes, halved

4 small sweet red cherry peppers (such as peppadew), thinly sliced

2 cloves garlic, thinly sliced

1 cup low-sodium chicken broth

1 Cook the orzo according to package directions. Drain and toss with the spinach and ¼ tsp each salt and pepper.

2 Meanwhile, heat 1 Tbsp oil in a large skillet over medium-high heat. Season the chicken with ½ tsp salt and ¼ tsp pepper. Cook 4 cutlets until browned and cooked through, 2 to 3 minutes per side; transfer to a plate and cover with foil to keep warm.

3 Heat the remaining Tbsp oil in the skillet. Cook the remaining cutlets for 2 minutes. Turn the cutlets and scatter the tomatoes, cherry peppers and garlic in the skillet. Cook until the chicken is golden brown and cooked through, 2 to 3 minutes more. Transfer the chicken to the plate.

4 Add the chicken broth to the skillet with the tomato mixture and bring to a simmer. Serve the chicken with the spinach orzo and top with the tomato mixture.

PER SERVING 416 CAL, 12 G FAT (2 G SAT FAT), 110 MG CHOL, 668 MG SOD, 44 G PRO, 32 G CAR, 4 G FIBER

Switch it up » For a vegetarian dinner, omit the chicken, use water or vegetable broth instead of chicken broth, double the spinach, and toss the tomato mixture with the orzo. Top with crumbled feta cheese before serving.

Asparagus and potato pizza

ACTIVE 15 MIN • **TOTAL** 35 MIN • **SERVES** 4 • **COST PER SERVING** $1.41

Cornmeal, for the baking sheet

1 lb pizza dough, thawed if frozen

2 medium Yukon Gold or other waxy potatoes (about 8 oz), thinly sliced

12 oz asparagus, trimmed and thinly sliced on the diagonal

½ red onion, thinly sliced

2 Tbsp olive oil

Kosher salt and pepper

2 oz thinly sliced provolone cheese (about 6 slices), halved

❶ Heat oven to 425°F. Dust a baking sheet with cornmeal. Shape the dough into a 16-in.-long oval or rectangle and place on the prepared baking sheet.

❷ In a large bowl, toss the potatoes, asparagus, onion, oil, ½ tsp salt and ¼ tsp pepper. Scatter the vegetables and cheese over the dough and bake until the potatoes are tender and the crust is golden brown and crisp, 20 to 25 minutes.

♥ **PER SERVING** 400 CAL, 15 G FAT (3 G SAT FAT), 13 MG CHOL, 688 MG SOD, 11 G PRO, 61 G CAR, 4 G FIBER

Prep tip » If the pizza dough shrinks back as you stretch it, let it rest for 10 minutes or so before trying to shape it again.

Pasta with roasted cauliflower and red onions

ACTIVE 15 MIN • **TOTAL** 30 MIN • **SERVES** 4
COST PER SERVING $1.99

- 1 small head cauliflower (about 1½ lb), cored and sliced ½ in. thick
- 1 red onion, cut into ½-in.-thick wedges
- ⅓ cup fresh sage, roughly chopped
- 2 Tbsp olive oil
-   Kosher salt and pepper
- ½ cup golden raisins
- 12 oz whole-grain penne
- ¼ cup grated Parmesan (1 oz), plus more for serving

❶ Heat oven to 425°F. On a rimmed baking sheet, toss the cauliflower, onion, sage, oil and ¼ tsp each salt and pepper; roast for 15 minutes. Add the raisins and toss to combine. Roast until the vegetables are golden brown and tender, 8 to 10 minutes more.

❷ Meanwhile, cook the pasta according to package directions. Drain the pasta and return it to the pot.

❸ Add the vegetable mixture and Parmesan to the pasta and toss to combine. Serve with additional Parmesan, if desired.

♥ **PER SERVING** 479 CAL, 10 G FAT (2 G SAT FAT), 4 MG CHOL, 259 MG SOD, 20 G PRO, 81 G CAR, 9 G FIBER

> ***Switch it up*** » Instead of pasta, serve the crispy roasted cauliflower with seared fish. Or scatter the raw cauliflower mixture over pizza dough, sprinkle with Parmesan and bake at 425°F until the vegetables are tender and the crust is golden brown and crisp, 20 to 25 minutes.

Roasted tilapia, tomatoes and garlic

ACTIVE 5 MIN • **TOTAL** 25 MIN • **SERVES** 4
COST PER SERVING $3.11

- 2 pint grape tomatoes
- 8 cloves garlic, smashed
- 2 Tbsp olive oil
  Kosher salt and black pepper
- 4 6-oz tilapia fillets
- ½ cup fresh flat-leaf parsley, chopped
- 1 Tbsp capers, roughly chopped

❶ Heat oven to 400°F. On a rimmed baking sheet or in a large roasting pan, toss the tomatoes, garlic, 1 Tbsp oil, ½ tsp salt and ¼ tsp pepper. Roast for 6 minutes.

❷ Nestle the fish among the tomatoes, drizzle with the remaining Tbsp oil, and season with ½ tsp salt and ¼ tsp pepper. Roast until the fish is opaque throughout and the tomatoes have begun to burst, 12 to 15 minutes.

❸ Transfer the fish to plates. Sprinkle the tomatoes with the parsley and capers, and toss to combine. Serve with the fish.

PER SERVING 518 CAL, 17 G FAT (3 G SAT FAT), 81 MG CHOL, 817 MG SOD, 47 G PRO, 54 G CAR, 10 G FIBER

Cook's tip » Double the roasted tomatoes and toss into spaghetti. For an easy appetizer, spread a sliced baguette with ricotta cheese and top with the roasted tomatoes.

Sweet and tangy glazed salmon with orange-almond rice

ACTIVE 20 MIN • **TOTAL** 25 MIN • **SERVES** 4 • **COST PER SERVING** $2.84

1	cup long-grain white rice
½	cup sliced almonds
2	navel oranges
½	cup hot pepper jelly
4	6-oz salmon steaks or skinless pieces salmon fillet
	Kosher salt and pepper
¼	cup fresh flat-leaf parsley, chopped

❶ Heat oven to 400°F. Cook the rice according to package directions.

❷ Meanwhile, spread the almonds on a rimmed baking sheet and roast until light golden brown, 4 to 6 minutes; transfer to a bowl. Heat broiler. Line a broiler-proof rimmed baking sheet with nonstick foil.

❸ Squeeze the juice from half an orange into a small bowl (you should have 2 Tbsp juice). Add the jelly and whisk to combine. Place the salmon on the baking sheet, season with ½ tsp each salt and pepper and broil for 5 minutes. Spoon half the jelly mixture over the salmon and broil until the salmon is opaque throughout, 2 to 5 minutes more.

❹ Cut away the peel and pith of the remaining 1½ oranges. Cut the oranges into ½-in. pieces. Fold the oranges, almonds and parsley into the rice. Serve with the salmon and the remaining jelly mixture.

....

♥ **PER SERVING** 555 CAL, 12 G FAT (2 G SAT FAT), 80 MG CHOL, 338 MG SOD, 41 G PRO, 68 G CAR, 3 G FIBER

Switch it up » Try this zesty jelly glaze on chicken breasts or boneless pork chops. Or use it as the sauce in your next stir-fry.

Orange-ginger chicken with spinach

ACTIVE 25 MIN • **TOTAL** 25 MIN • **SERVES** 4
COST PER SERVING $1.73

- 1 large orange
- 3 Tbsp olive oil
- 4 6-oz boneless, skinless chicken breasts
  Kosher salt and pepper
- 1 1½-in. piece fresh ginger, peeled and thinly sliced into matchsticks
- ½ cup orange marmalade
- 1 Tbsp cider vinegar
- 2 scallions, thinly sliced
- 3 cloves garlic, thinly sliced
- 1 11-oz pkg spinach, thick stems discarded
  Toasted sesame seeds, for serving

❶ Cut away the peel and white pith of the orange. Working over a bowl, cut the orange into segments, adding them to the bowl along with any juices.

❷ Heat 1 Tbsp oil in a large skillet over medium heat. Season the chicken with ½ tsp each salt and pepper; cook until golden brown and cooked through, 6 to 8 minutes per side; transfer to a plate.

❸ Wipe out the skillet; heat 1 Tbsp oil over medium heat. Sauté the ginger for 1 minute. Add the marmalade and cook, stirring, until melted. Add the vinegar and the oranges (and any juices) to the skillet; cook until heated through, about 2 minutes. Return the chicken to the skillet, sprinkle with the scallions; turn to coat.

❹ Heat the remaining Tbsp oil in a second skillet over medium heat. Add the garlic and cook, stirring occasionally, until golden brown, about 2 minutes. Add the spinach, season with ½ tsp salt and ¼ tsp pepper and cook, tossing, until beginning to wilt, about 2 minutes. Transfer the spinach to plates; sprinkle with the sesame seeds, if desired. Serve with the chicken.

PER SERVING 398 CAL, 13 G FAT (2 G SAT FAT), 94 MG CHOL, 629 MG SOD, 37 G PRO, 36 G CAR, 3 G FIBER

> *Love your leftovers »* Make a tasty next-day lunch: Thinly slice any leftover chicken. Warm a French baguette and split. Lay the sliced chicken on the baguette and top with leftover spinach and orange mixture. Alternately, roll up in a large flour tortilla.

Sweet potato flatbread

ACTIVE 15 MIN • **TOTAL** 40 MIN • **SERVES** 4
COST PER SERVING $1.43

Cornmeal, for the baking sheet

1 lb pizza dough, thawed if frozen

1 medium sweet potato, peeled, halved and thinly sliced

2 shallots, thinly sliced

4 oz extra-sharp Cheddar, coarsely grated

1 Tbsp fresh thyme

¼ cup slivered almonds

2 Tbsp olive oil

Kosher salt and pepper

Green salad, for serving

❶ Heat oven to 425°F. Dust a baking sheet with cornmeal. Shape the dough into a 14-in.-long rectangle or oval and place on the prepared baking sheet.

❷ In a large bowl, toss the sweet potato, shallots, Cheddar, thyme, almonds, oil, ½ tsp salt and ¼ tsp pepper. Scatter the potato mixture over the dough and bake until golden brown and crisp, 20 to 25 minutes. Serve with the salad, if desired.

PER SERVING 524 CAL, 18 G FAT (4 G SAT FAT), 30 MG CHOL, 1,012 MG SOD, 20 G PRO, 65 G CAR, 2 G FIBER

Switch it up » Replace the sweet potato with butternut squash and use a small red onion instead of shallots.

Buttermilk chicken and cornflake bake

ACTIVE 30 MIN • **TOTAL** 1 HR • **SERVES** 8 • **COST PER SERVING** $1.08

2	lb boneless, skinless chicken breasts, cut into 1-in. pieces	½	cup orange juice
2	Tbsp olive oil	1	14.5-oz can low-sodium chicken broth
2	large carrots, cut into ¼-in. pieces	1	cup frozen peas, thawed
1	large onion, chopped Kosher salt	2	Tbsp roughly chopped fresh dill
1	tsp Cajun or blackening seasoning	½	cup fresh flat-leaf parsley, chopped
¼	cup all-purpose flour	½	cup buttermilk
		2½	cups cornflakes

❶ Heat oven to 375°F. Place the chicken in a large pot, cover with water and bring to a boil (about 10 minutes). Transfer the chicken to a plate and set aside.

❷ Meanwhile, heat the oil in a large skillet over medium heat. Add the carrots, onion and ½ tsp salt and cook, covered, stirring occasionally, until tender, 8 to 10 minutes; stir in the Cajun seasoning.

❸ Sprinkle the flour over the vegetables and cook, stirring, for 1 minute. Gradually stir in the orange juice, then the broth and bring to a boil. Add the chicken, peas, dill and half the parsley and stir to combine. Remove from heat and stir in the buttermilk.

❹ Transfer the mixture to a 2½- to 3-qt baking dish and bake for 15 minutes. In a medium bowl, combine the cornflakes and the remaining parsley. Sprinkle over the chicken mixture and bake for 5 minutes more. Let stand for 10 minutes before serving.

♥ **PER SERVING** 258 CAL, 7 G FAT (1 G SAT FAT), 68 MG CHOL, 353 MG SOD, 29 G PRO, 20 G CAR, 2 G FIBER

Make ahead » Prepare the chicken mixture and refrigerate for up to 2 days. When ready to cook, transfer the mixture to a casserole dish and reheat, covered, in a 375°F oven for 20 minutes. Top with the cornflakes and continue to bake as directed.

Stuffed peppers with white beans

ACTIVE 25 MIN • **TOTAL** 30 MIN • **SERVES** 4 • **COST PER SERVING** $3.04

- 4 bell peppers
- 2 Tbsp olive oil
- Kosher salt and pepper
- 1 large onion, chopped
- 3 cloves garlic, finely chopped
- 1 10-oz pkg fresh spinach, thick stems discarded, leaves roughly chopped

- 1 15-oz can small white beans, rinsed
- 2 Tbsp fresh lemon juice
- 4 oz part-skim mozzarella, coarsely grated (about 1 cup)
- ¼ cup grated Parmesan (1 oz)
- 1 cup marinara sauce

❶ Heat broiler. Cut the peppers in half lengthwise; discard the seeds. On a rimmed baking sheet, toss the peppers with 1 Tbsp oil and ¼ tsp each salt and pepper. Arrange cut-side down and broil for 3 minutes. Turn and broil until beginning to soften, 3 minutes more. Pour off any accumulated liquid. Reduce the oven temperature to 425°F.

❷ Meanwhile, heat the remaining Tbsp oil in a large skillet over medium heat. Add the onion and cook, covered, stirring occasionally, until tender, 5 to 6 minutes. Stir in the garlic and cook for 1 minute.

❸ Add the spinach and ¼ tsp each salt and pepper to the skillet and cook, tossing, until beginning to wilt, 1 to 2 minutes. Remove from heat and fold in the beans and lemon juice, then the mozzarella and Parmesan.

❹ Spread the marinara sauce on the bottom of a 9 x 13-in. baking dish. Dividing evenly, fill the peppers with the bean mixture (about ½ cup each), then place on top of the sauce in the baking dish. Bake until the peppers are tender and the cheese has melted, 4 to 6 minutes.

Flavor boost » For a little kick, add 1 small red chili (thinly sliced) or ¼ to ½ tsp crushed red pepper flakes to the skillet along with the garlic.

PER SERVING 313 CAL, 14 G FAT (4 G SAT FAT), 18 MG CHOL, 966 MG SOD, 16 G PRO, 36 G CAR, 12 G FIBER

Pierogies with sautéed cabbage and bacon

ACTIVE 20 MIN • **TOTAL** 20 MIN • **SERVES** 4 • **COST PER SERVING** $1.21

1   16-oz box frozen potato and onion pierogies

4   slices bacon

1   Tbsp olive oil

1   medium onion, thinly sliced

½   small green cabbage (about lb), cored and thinly sliced

   Kosher salt and pepper

1   Tbsp whole-grain mustard

1   Tbsp prepared horseradish

¼   cup fresh flat-leaf parsley, chopped

❶ Cook the pierogies according to package directions.

❷ Meanwhile, cook the bacon in a large skillet over medium heat until crisp, about 5 minutes. Transfer to a paper towel–lined plate; break into pieces when cool.

❸ Wipe out the skillet and heat the oil over medium heat. Add the onion and cook, covered, stirring occasionally, for 4 minutes. Add the cabbage, season with ¼ tsp each salt and pepper and cook, covered, stirring occasionally, until the vegetables are just tender, 2 to 3 minutes.

❹ Stir in the mustard, horseradish and 1 Tbsp water and cook for 1 minute. Fold in the bacon and parsley and serve with the pierogies.

💚 **PER SERVING** 273 CAL, 9 G FAT (2 G SAT FAT), 14 MG CHOL, 771 MG SOD, 10 G PRO, 41 G CAR, 4 G FIBER

Easy side » The sautéed cabbage and bacon mixture is a delicious accompaniment to seared fish or chicken.

Halibut with spinach, oranges and olives

ACTIVE 20 MIN • **TOTAL** 20 MIN • **SERVES** 4
COST PER SERVING $4.26

2	Tbsp olive oil
4	6-oz pieces skinless halibut or cod fillet
	Kosher salt and pepper
1	Tbsp white wine vinegar
2	tsp honey
1	navel orange
¼	sweet onion, thinly sliced
¼	cup pitted green olives, sliced
1	bunch spinach, thick stems removed (about 4 cups)

1 Heat 1 Tbsp oil in a large skillet over medium-high heat. Season the halibut with ½ tsp salt and ¼ tsp pepper and cook until golden brown and opaque throughout, 3 to 5 minutes per side.

2 In a large bowl, whisk together the vinegar, honey, remaining Tbsp oil and ¼ tsp each salt and pepper.

3 Cut away the peel and white pith of the orange and slice into rounds. Add them to the bowl along with the onion, olives and spinach, and gently toss to combine. Serve with the halibut.

PER SERVING 297 CAL, 11 G FAT (1 G SAT FAT), 58 MG CHOL, 602 MG SOD, 39 G PRO, 11 G CAR, 2 G FIBER

Cook's tip » Halibut is a meaty and flavorsome fish, but you can save up to $4 per pound by using tilapia, cod or hake instead.

Lo mein with pork and vegetables

ACTIVE 25 MIN • **TOTAL** 30 MIN • **SERVES** 4
COST PER SERVING $1.49

- 8 oz udon noodles or linguine
- ¼ cup tomato purée (no added salt)
- 2 Tbsp rice vinegar
- 2 Tbsp dark brown sugar
- ¼ tsp cayenne pepper
- 2 tsp toasted sesame oil (optional)
- 1 Tbsp plus 2 tsp canola oil
- 8 oz ground pork
- 4 oz shiitake mushrooms, stems discarded, caps sliced, or white mushrooms, sliced
- ½ lb medium carrots (about 2), cut into matchsticks
- 4 cloves garlic, finely chopped
- 1 1-in. piece fresh ginger, finely chopped
- 1 medium zucchini, cut into matchsticks
- ½ small Napa cabbage (about ½ lb), sliced into ½-in.-thick strips

1 In a large pot, cook the noodles according to package directions. In a small bowl, whisk together the tomato purée, vinegar, sugar, cayenne, sesame oil (if using) and ¼ cup water. Drain the noodles, return them to the pot and toss with the tomato mixture.

2 Meanwhile, heat 2 tsp canola oil in a large nonstick skillet over medium-high heat. Add the pork and cook, breaking it up with a spoon, until browned, 4 to 5 minutes; transfer to a bowl.

3 Wipe out the skillet and heat the remaining Tbsp canola oil. Add the mushrooms and cook, tossing, for 2 minutes. Add the carrots, garlic and ginger and cook, tossing, for 1 minute. Add the zucchini and cabbage and cook, tossing occasionally, until the cabbage begins to wilt, about 2 minutes.

4 Return the pork to the skillet and toss to combine. Toss the vegetable mixture with the noodle mixture.

♥ **PER SERVING** 503 CAL, 20 G FAT (5 G SAT FAT), 41 MG CHOL, 173 MG SOD, 20 G PRO, 61 G CAR, 7 G FIBER

Cook's tip » Udon noodles are thick wheat noodles with a hearty, chewy texture. They're often used for soups but are also delicious in stir-fries.

Roasted salmon, green beans and tomatoes

ACTIVE 15 MIN • **TOTAL** 20 MIN • **SERVES** 4 • **COST PER SERVING** $3.65

6 cloves garlic, smashed

1 lb green beans, trimmed

1 pint grape tomatoes

½ cup pitted Kalamata olives

3 anchovy fillets, chopped (optional)

2 Tbsp olive oil

   Kosher salt and pepper

1 1¼-lb skinless salmon fillet, cut into 4 pieces

❶ Heat oven to 425°F. On a large rimmed baking sheet, toss together the garlic, beans, tomatoes, olives and anchovies (if using) with 1 Tbsp oil and ¼ tsp pepper. Roast until the vegetables are tender and beginning to brown, 12 to 15 minutes.

❷ Meanwhile, heat the remaining Tbsp oil in a large skillet over medium heat. Season the salmon with ¼ tsp each salt and pepper and cook until golden brown and opaque throughout, 4 to 5 minutes per side. Serve with the vegetables.

♥ **PER SERVING** 306 CAL, 15 G FAT (3 G SAT FAT), 66 MG CHOL, 445 MG SOD, 31 G PRO, 13 G CAR, 4 G FIBER

Cook's tip » Anchovies are a secret ingredient in this dish. They dissolve while cooking, leaving a slight salty and delicious flavor without a fishy taste.

Parsley pasta with sautéed artichokes

ACTIVE 25 MIN • **TOTAL** 25 MIN • **SERVES** 4 • **COST PER SERVING** $2.63

12	oz whole-wheat penne
2	Tbsp olive oil
4	cloves garlic, finely chopped
1	red chili (seeded if desired), thinly sliced, or ¼ to ½ tsp crushed red pepper flakes
1	anchovy fillet, finely chopped (optional)
1	16-oz pkg frozen artichokes, thawed, patted dry and roughly chopped
½	cup dry white wine
2	tsp lemon zest plus 2 Tbsp juice
1	large bunch fresh flat-leaf parsley, stems discarded (about 3½ cups leaves), chopped
2	Tbsp grated Parmesan

❶ Cook the penne according to package directions.

❷ Meanwhile, in a large nonstick skillet, heat the oil over medium heat. Add the garlic, chili and anchovy (if using) and cook, stirring, until the garlic is tender and beginning to brown, 1 to 2 minutes.

❸ Add the artichokes to the pan, increase the heat to medium-high and cook, tossing occasionally, until golden brown, about 3 minutes. Add the wine, lemon zest and juice and simmer for 2 minutes.

❹ Stir in the parsley and cook for 1 minute. Toss the artichoke mixture with the pasta and top with the Parmesan.

♥ **PER SERVING** 490 CAL, 12.5 G FAT (2 G SAT FAT), 4 MG CHOL, 199 MG SOD, 17 G PRO, 80 G CAR, 16 G FIBER

Cook's tip » Use this zesty artichoke mixture as an appetizer. Toast a thinly sliced baguette until golden brown, then top with the artichoke mixture and Parmesan.

Orange-ginger turkey meat loaf

ACTIVE 15 MIN • **TOTAL** 55 MIN • **SERVES** 4 • **COST PER SERVING** $2.99

1   orange

1   large egg white

1   Tbsp grated fresh ginger

2   cloves garlic, finely chopped

     Kosher salt and pepper

½   cup whole-wheat bread crumbs

1   medium carrot, coarsely grated

½   cup fresh cilantro, roughly chopped, plus 1 cup leaves

4   scallions, thinly sliced

1¼   lb lean ground turkey (preferably white meat)

2   Tbsp hoisin sauce

2   Tbsp ketchup

6   cups mixed greens

1   Tbsp olive oil

Make ahead » Shape the meat mixture into a loaf, wrap tightly in foil and freeze for up to 3 months. Thaw in the refrigerator overnight. Place on a foil-lined baking sheet and bake and glaze as directed.

1 Heat oven to 375°F. Line a rimmed baking sheet with foil. Using a vegetable peeler, remove 2 strips of zest from the orange and very thinly slice on a diagonal; transfer the zest to a large bowl and set the orange aside.

2 Add the egg white, ginger, garlic, 1 Tbsp water and ½ tsp each salt and pepper to the bowl with the zest and whisk to combine; stir in the bread crumbs. Add the carrot, chopped cilantro and half the scallions, and mix to combine.

3 Add the turkey and mix just until incorporated. Transfer the mixture to the prepared baking sheet, shape into a 9 x 3½-in. loaf and bake for 25 minutes. In a small bowl, combine the hoisin and ketchup. Brush the mixture over the entire loaf and bake until the internal temperature registers 160°F, 10 to 15 minutes more. Let rest for 5 minutes before slicing.

4 While the meat loaf is resting, cut away the peel and white pith of the orange and thinly slice into rounds. In a large bowl, gently toss the orange slices, greens, oil, cilantro leaves, remaining scallions and ¼ tsp each salt and pepper. Serve with the meat loaf.

♥ PER SERVING 300 CAL, 6 G FAT (1 G SAT FAT), 83 MG CHOL, 715 MG SOD, 44 G PRO, 20 G CAR, 5 G FIBER

Arugula, sweet potato and spiced steak salad

ACTIVE 20 MIN • **TOTAL** 25 MIN • **SERVES** 4 • **COST PER SERVING** $2.27

1	12-oz, 1-in.-thick piece sirloin or top round steak (London broil)
1	tsp ground cumin
	Kosher salt and pepper
1	Tbsp olive oil
1½	lb sweet potatoes, peeled and cut into 1-in. pieces
1	clove garlic, finely chopped

1	lime
½	cup fresh flat-leaf parsley, chopped
3	scallions, finely chopped
1	5-oz pkg baby arugula or mixed greens
2	cups fresh cilantro leaves (optional)

1 Heat broiler and line a rimmed baking sheet with nonstick foil.

2 Season the steak with the cumin and ½ tsp each salt and pepper and broil to desired doneness, 7 to 8 minutes per side for medium-rare. Transfer to a cutting board and let rest for at least 5 minutes before slicing.

3 Meanwhile, place the oil and ¾ cup water in a large nonstick skillet and bring to a simmer. Add the sweet potatoes, toss to coat, cover and cook, stirring twice, for 4 minutes. Remove the cover and cook until golden brown and just barely tender, about 5 minutes.

4 Add the garlic to the pan and cook, tossing, for 1 minute; remove from the heat. Grate the zest of 1 lime over the potatoes, then squeeze the juice over the mixture. Sprinkle with the parsley, scallions and ¼ tsp each salt and pepper; toss to coat.

5 In a large bowl, toss together the arugula and cilantro (if using), then the sweet potatoes and sliced steak.

Love your leftovers » Make a quick burrito: Roll leftovers in a tortilla with grated Cheddar and rinsed canned black beans.

PER SERVING 290 CAL, 10 G FAT (3 G SAT FAT), 55 MG CHOL, 452 MG SOD, 22 G PRO, 29 G CAR, 5 G FIBER

Turkey Bolognese

ACTIVE 40 MIN • **TOTAL** 50 MIN • **SERVES** 4 • **COST PER SERVING** $2.07

2	Tbsp olive oil
1	onion, chopped
2	stalks celery, chopped
3	cloves garlic, finely chopped
2	tsp dried thyme
2	tsp dried oregano
1	small cinnamon stick
	Kosher salt and pepper
1¼	lb lean ground turkey
3	cups low-sodium marinara sauce
12	oz whole-wheat linguine
⅛	tsp ground nutmeg
	Chopped fresh basil and grated Parmesan, for serving

1 Heat the oil in a large skillet over medium heat. Add the onion, celery and garlic; cook, covered, stirring occasionally, for 6 minutes. Add the thyme, oregano, cinnamon and ¼ tsp each salt and pepper; cook, stirring, for 1 minute.

2 Add the turkey and cook, breaking it up with a spoon until no longer pink, about 5 minutes. Add the marinara sauce and ½ cup water and simmer until the mixture is slightly thickened and the turkey tender, 20 to 25 minutes.

3 Meanwhile, cook the pasta according to package directions. Drain the pasta and return it to the pot.

4 Discard the cinnamon from the turkey mixture, stir in the nutmeg and toss with the pasta. Serve with basil and Parmesan, if desired.

PER SERVING 589 CAL, 12.5 G FAT (2 G SAT FAT), 78 MG CHOL, 376 MG SOD, 48 G PRO, 77 G CAR, 9 G FIBER

Make ahead » Freeze the Bolognese for up to 3 months. Thaw in the fridge overnight and reheat in a medium saucepan, covered, stirring occasionally. Cook the pasta according to package directions, reserving some of the cooking water. Toss the pasta with the Bolognese, adding some of the reserved pasta water if it seems too thick.

Seafood, chorizo and vegetable stew

ACTIVE 15 MIN • **TOTAL** 20 MIN • **SERVES** 4 • **COST PER SERVING** $3.83

1   Tbsp olive oil

2   oz Spanish chorizo
    (fully cooked and cured),
    thinly sliced

2   stalks celery, thinly sliced

1   bulb fennel, cored and
    thinly sliced

2   cloves garlic, thinly sliced

1   28-oz can whole peeled
    tomatoes in juice

¾   cup dry white wine

1   12-oz cod fillet, cut into
    2-in. pieces

½   lb large peeled and
    deveined shrimp

1   Tbsp red wine vinegar

1   Tbsp fresh tarragon, chopped

    Crusty bread, for serving

❶ Heat the oil in a large pot or Dutch oven over medium-high heat. Add the chorizo and cook, stirring, for 1 minute.

❷ Add the celery, fennel and garlic and cook, covered, stirring occasionally, until beginning to soften, 3 to 4 minutes.

❸ Crush the tomatoes and add to the pan along with their juices. Add the wine and bring to a boil. Add the cod and shrimp and cook, covered, stirring once, until opaque throughout, 3 to 4 minutes. Remove from heat and stir in the vinegar and tarragon. Serve with bread, if desired.

PER SERVING 279 CAL, 10 G FAT (3 G SAT FAT), 120 MG CHOL, 1,023 MG SOD, 29 G PRO, 16 G CAR, 4 G FIBER

Prep tip » To prepare fennel, trim off the darker green stalks, reserving any delicate fronts for garnish if desired. Slice off the tough root end (about ½-in. from the bottom) and slice in half from top to bottom. Cut out and discard the tough core. Slice to desired thickness. The green stalks are fine to eat, but slice thinly as their flavor is stronger.

Tortilla-crusted fish sticks with slaw

ACTIVE 20 MIN • **TOTAL** 25 MIN • **SERVES** 4
COST PER SERVING $2.64

1	navel orange
2	Tbsp fresh lime juice
2	tsp sugar
	Kosher salt and pepper
½	cup sour cream
2	carrots, coarsely grated
½	small cabbage (about 1 lb), chopped
1½	lb tilapia fillets
3	cups tortilla chips, crushed

❶ Heat oven to 425°F. Finely grate 1 tsp of zest from the orange into a large bowl, then squeeze in the juice (about ½ cup). Add the lime juice, sugar, ¾ tsp salt and ½ tsp pepper and whisk until the sugar dissolves; whisk in the sour cream. Transfer ½ cup of the mixture to a shallow bowl; whisk in ¼ tsp each salt and pepper and set aside.

❷ Add the carrots and cabbage to the large bowl and let sit, tossing occasionally, for 15 minutes.

❸ Meanwhile, line a rimmed baking sheet with foil. Cut the tilapia diagonally into 1½-in.-thick strips. Dip the fish in the reserved sour cream mixture and then in the chips, pressing gently to help them adhere. Transfer the fish sticks to the baking sheet and roast until light golden brown and opaque throughout, 8 to 10 minutes. Serve with the slaw.

PER SERVING 349 CAL, 12 G FAT (4 G SAT FAT), 87 MG CHOL, 635 MG SOD, 39 G PRO, 25 G CAR, 5 G FIBER

Switch it up » For a colorful variation, use a mixture of white, yellow and blue corn tortilla chips for the coating.

Chickpea, orange and tomato salad

ACTIVE 15 MIN • **TOTAL** 15 MIN • **SERVES** 4
COST PER SERVING $1.66

- 1   navel orange
- 1   cup couscous
- 1   lb cherry tomatoes, halved
- 1   15-oz can chickpeas, rinsed
- ½   small sweet onion, thinly sliced
- ½   cup pitted green olives, halved
- 1   Tbsp olive oil
-     Kosher salt and pepper

❶ Grate 2 tsp orange zest into a medium bowl. Add the couscous and toss to combine. Add 1 cup tap water, cover and let stand for 12 minutes; fluff with a fork.

❷ Meanwhile, cut away the peel and pith of the orange. Working over a large bowl, cut out the segments, adding them to the bowl as you go. Squeeze the juice of the remaining membrane into the bowl.

❸ Add the tomatoes, chickpeas, onion, olives, oil, ½ tsp salt and ¼ tsp pepper, and gently mix to combine. Serve over the couscous.

♥ **PER SERVING** 350 CAL, 8 G FAT (1 G SAT FAT), 0 MG CHOL, 726 MG SOD, 12 G PRO, 59 G CAR, 9 G FIBER

Prep tip » To prepare the orange, use a sharp knife to slice off a small piece from the top and bottom. Stand it up on one of the cut ends and cut away the remaining peel and white pith.

Linguine with tomatoes, spinach and clams

ACTIVE 25 MIN • **TOTAL** 25 MIN • **SERVES** 4 • **COST PER SERVING** $2.22

12	oz linguine
¼	cup olive oil
6	cloves garlic, finely chopped
½	tsp crushed red pepper flakes
1	14.5-oz can whole peeled tomatoes
¾	cup dry white wine
2	6.5-oz cans chopped clams, drained
½	cup fresh flat-leaf parsley, roughly chopped
1	bunch spinach, thick stems discarded
	Grated Parmesan, for serving

1 Cook the pasta according to package directions. Drain and return it to the pot.

2 Meanwhile, heat the oil, garlic and red pepper flakes in a large skillet over medium heat, stirring occasionally, until the garlic is fragrant, 2 to 3 minutes.

3 Crush the tomatoes and add them to the skillet along with their juices. Add the wine and clams and simmer, stirring occasionally, for 5 minutes. Stir in the parsley.

4 Toss the pasta with the spinach and sauce. Serve with Parmesan, if desired.

PER SERVING 571 CAL, 16 G FAT (2 G SAT FAT), 32 MG CHOL, 355 MG SOD, 30 G PRO, 76 G CAR, 5 G FIBER

Use up the linguine and Parmesan » Cook the remaining 4 oz linguine; roughly chop and refrigerate. Beat 4 eggs and toss with the pasta, chopped scallion and grated Parmesan. Cook in olive oil in a nonstick skillet over medium heat until the bottom is golden brown, 10 minutes. Flip and cook 2 minutes more.

Kale, white bean, chicken and butternut squash soup

ACTIVE 25 MIN • **TOTAL** 30 MIN • **SERVES** 4 • **COST PER SERVING** $3.65

- 1   2½- to 3-lb rotisserie chicken
- 2   Tbsp olive oil
- 1   large onion, chopped
      Kosher salt and pepper
- 2   stalks celery, thinly sliced
- 3   cloves garlic, finely chopped
- 6   sprigs fresh thyme
- 2   Tbsp tomato paste
- 1   medium butternut squash (about 1 lb), peeled, seeded and cut into ½-in. pieces
- 1   bunch kale (about 1 lb), stems and large ribs discarded, leaves chopped
- 1   15-oz can low-sodium white beans, rinsed

❶ Remove and discard the skin from the rotisserie chicken. Shred the meat into a bowl and set aside. Place the carcass and bones in a medium pot. Add 8 cups water, cover and bring to a boil. Reduce heat and simmer for 15 minutes.

❷ Meanwhile, heat the oil in a large pot over medium heat. Add the onion, season with ¾ tsp salt and ½ tsp pepper and cook, covered, stirring occasionally, for 8 minutes. Add the celery, garlic and thyme and cook, stirring occasionally, until the onion is lightly golden brown around the edges, 4 to 6 minutes. Add the tomato paste and cook, stirring, for 1 minute.

❸ Strain the chicken mixture into the vegetable mixture and discard the bones. Add the squash and bring to a boil. Reduce heat and simmer until the squash is just tender, 5 to 7 minutes. Stir in the kale, beans and chicken. Cook, stirring, until the kale is just tender, about 3 minutes. Discard the thyme sprigs before serving.

💙 **PER SERVING** 262 CAL, 10 G FAT (2 G SAT FAT), 68 MG CHOL, 568 MG SOD, 25 G PRO, 21 G CAR, 5 G FIBER

Prep tip » To quickly separate kale leaves from the stem, hold the kale by the stem end, and remove the leaf by pulling it downward.

Seared fish with artichoke relish

ACTIVE 20 MIN • **TOTAL** 30 MIN • **SERVES** 4 • **COST PER SERVING** $2.96

3	Tbsp olive oil
1	medium onion, finely chopped
	Kosher salt and pepper
2	stalks celery, finely chopped
2	cloves garlic, finely chopped
1	14-oz can artichoke hearts, rinsed, patted dry and roughly chopped
¼	cup pitted green olives, quartered
1	Tbsp red wine vinegar
½	cup fresh flat-leaf parsley, roughly chopped
¼	cup roasted almonds, chopped
4	6-oz pieces skinless white fish fillets (such as cod, striped bass, halibut or tilapia)
1	cup couscous
¼	cup tomato sauce

1 Heat 1 Tbsp oil in a large skillet over medium heat. Add the onion, ½ tsp salt and ¼ tsp pepper and cook, covered, stirring occasionally, for 6 minutes. Add the celery and garlic and cook, covered, stirring occasionally, for 3 minutes.

2 Add the artichokes, olives, vinegar and 1 Tbsp oil and mix to combine. Fold in the parsley and almonds. Transfer the artichoke relish to a bowl.

3 Wipe out the skillet and heat the remaining Tbsp oil over medium-high heat. Season the fish with ½ tsp each salt and pepper and cook until golden brown and opaque throughout, 3 to 5 minutes per side (depending on type of fish and size of fillets).

4 Meanwhile, place the couscous in a bowl. Stir in 1 cup boiling water, then the tomato sauce. Cover and let sit for 5 minutes, then fluff with a fork. Serve the fish and relish with the couscous.

....

♥ **PER SERVING** 483 CAL, 15 G FAT (2 G SAT FAT), 65 MG CHOL, 798 MG SOD, 37 G PRO, 47 G CAR, 5 G FIBER

Switch it up » This flavorful artichoke relish also goes nicely with seared lamb chops, grilled chicken breasts or broiled steak.

Classic minestrone

ACTIVE 25 MIN • **TOTAL** 45 MIN • **SERVES** 6
COST PER SERVING $1.61

- 2 Tbsp olive oil, plus more for serving
- 1 large onion, chopped
  Kosher salt and pepper
- 2 large cloves garlic, finely chopped
- 2 Tbsp tomato paste
- 4 carrots, peeled and sliced ¼ in. thick
- 2 stalks celery, sliced ¼ in. thick
- 1 russet potato, peeled and cut into ½-in. pieces

- 6 sprigs fresh thyme (optional)
- ½ small head savoy cabbage, cored, quartered and cut into 1-in.-thick strips
- 1 cup ditalini pasta
- 1 15.5-oz can white beans, rinsed
- 2 cups baby spinach
  Parmesan cheese and crusty bread, for serving

❶ Heat the oil in a large pot over medium heat. Add the onion, season with ¼ tsp each salt and pepper and cook, covered, stirring occasionally, until very tender, 8 to 10 minutes. Stir in the garlic and cook for 1 minute. Add the tomato paste and cook, stirring, for 2 minutes.

❷ Add the carrots, celery, potato, thyme (if using) and 8 cups water and bring to a boil. Reduce heat and simmer for 10 minutes. Add the cabbage and simmer until the vegetables are tender, 10 to 12 minutes more.

❸ Meanwhile, cook the pasta according to package directions.

❹ Discard the thyme. Stir the pasta and beans into the soup and cook until the beans are heated through, about 3 minutes. Remove from heat and add the spinach, folding until beginning to wilt. Serve with additional olive oil, Parmesan and crusty bread, if desired.

Flavor boost » Add leftover Parmesan rinds to the soup at the beginning. They lend a subtle cheesy taste as the soup simmers.

♥ **PER SERVING** 264 CAL, 5 G FAT (1 G SAT FAT), 0 MG CHOL, 567 MG SOD, 10 G PRO, 46 G CAR, 8 G FIBER

One-pan spring chicken with asparagus and edamame

ACTIVE 30 MIN • **TOTAL** 30 MIN • **SERVES** 4 • **COST PER SERVING** $3.01

3	Tbsp all-purpose flour
	Kosher salt and pepper
4	6-oz boneless, skinless chicken breasts
2	Tbsp olive oil
1	small red onion, thinly sliced
1	clove garlic, finely chopped
½	cup white wine
1	cup low-sodium chicken broth
1	lb medium asparagus, sliced ¼ in. thick on a diagonal
1	cup frozen edamame, thawed
2	Tbsp fresh dill, chopped
1	Tbsp sour cream
1	Tbsp fresh lemon juice
	Steamed new potatoes or crusty bread, for serving

1 In a shallow bowl or pie dish, whisk together the flour and ½ tsp each salt and pepper. Coat the chicken breasts in the flour mixture.

2 Heat the oil in a large skillet over medium-high heat and cook the chicken breasts until golden brown on one side, 4 to 6 minutes. Turn the chicken, add the onion and garlic and cook, stirring the onion and garlic occasionally, for 3 minutes.

3 Add the wine to the skillet and simmer, scraping up any brown bits, until reduced by half, 1 to 2 minutes. Add the broth, return to a boil, then reduce heat and simmer until the chicken is cooked through, 5 to 6 minutes more.

4 Two minutes before the chicken is done, add the asparagus and edamame to the skillet and cook, stirring occasionally, until just tender.

5 Remove from heat and stir in the dill, sour cream and lemon juice. Serve with potatoes or crusty bread, if desired.

PER SERVING 361 CAL, 14 G FAT (2.5 G SAT FAT), 110 MG CHOL, 477 MG SOD, 44 G PRO, 15 G CAR, 4 G FIBER

Switch it up » Substitute 4 small bone-in pork chops for the chicken. Cook until golden brown on one side, 6 to 8 minutes, then turn, add the onion and garlic and cook as directed.

Pineapple and ham fried rice

ACTIVE 30 MIN • **TOTAL** 30 MIN • **SERVES** 4 • **COST PER SERVING** $1.18

1 cup long-grain white rice

1 Tbsp vegetable oil

6 oz thick-cut sliced ham, cut into thin ½-in. pieces

1 lb pineapple (about ¼ medium), peeled, cored and cut into thin ½-in. pieces

1 large red pepper, quartered and thinly sliced

1 medium red onion, thinly sliced

1 jalapeño (seeded for less heat, if desired), thinly sliced

1 1-in. piece fresh ginger, peeled, cut into ½-in. matchsticks

2 large cloves garlic, finely chopped

Chopped fresh cilantro and lime wedges, for serving

❶ Cook the rice according to package directions.

❷ Meanwhile, heat the oil in a large nonstick skillet over medium heat. Add the ham and cook, tossing occasionally, until beginning to brown, about 3 minutes. Add the pineapple and cook until beginning to brown around the edges, 3 to 4 minutes.

❸ Add the pepper and cook, tossing, for 2 minutes. Add the onion and cook, tossing, for 3 minutes. Add the jalapeño, ginger and garlic and cook, tossing occasionally, until the vegetables are just tender, 2 to 3 minutes more.

❹ Add the cooked rice to the skillet and cook tossing for 2 minutes. Serve with cilantro and lime wedges, if desired.

PER SERVING 326 CAL, 6 G FAT (.5 G SAT FAT), 23 MG CHOL, 476 MG SOD, 13 G PRO, 57 G CAR, 2 G FIBER

Cook's tip » For fried rice with the best texture, cook the rice the day before and cool in the fridge. Or, after cooking the rice, spread out on a rimmed baking sheet to cool as much as possible before adding to the skillet. This will keep the grains from sticking together.

Side Dishes

Pair any of these tasty sides with your favorite chicken, pork or fish to make an ordinary Tuesday night dinner feel exciting and new.

Mustard-glazed Brussels sprouts with chestnuts

ACTIVE 25 MIN • **TOTAL** 25 MIN • **SERVES** 8 • COST PER SERVING 86¢

- 4   Tbsp olive oil
- 2   lb (small) Brussels sprouts, trimmed and halved lengthwise
     Kosher salt and pepper
- ⅓   cup apricot jam
- 3   Tbsp white wine vinegar
- 1   Tbsp whole-grain mustard
- 4   cloves garlic, thinly sliced
- ½   cup jarred chestnuts, sliced

❶ Bring ½ cup water and 2 Tbsp oil to a simmer in a large skillet. Add the Brussels sprouts, season with ½ tsp salt, and cook, covered, stirring occasionally, for 5 minutes.

❷ Meanwhile, in a small bowl, whisk together the jam, vinegar, mustard and ½ tsp pepper.

❸ Uncover, increase the heat to medium-high, and cook until the water evaporates, about 2 minutes. Drizzle the remaining 2 Tbsp oil over the sprouts, add the garlic and cook, tossing occasionally, until the Brussels sprouts are golden brown and tender, 2 to 3 minutes.

❹ Add the jam mixture and the chestnuts and cook for 1 minute.

PER SERVING 161 CAL, 7 G FAT (1 G SAT FAT), 0 MG CHOL, 174 MG SOD, 4 G PRO, 23 G CAR, 4 G FIBER

Make ahead » Prepare the Brussels sprouts without the chestnuts. Refrigerate for up to 1 day. To serve, reheat in a large skillet over medium heat. Toss with the chestnuts before serving.

Green beans with toasted garlic and almonds

ACTIVE 15 MIN • **TOTAL** 15 MIN • **SERVES** 8 • COST PER SERVING 35¢

Kosher salt and pepper
2 lb green beans, trimmed
3 Tbsp olive oil
2 cloves garlic, thinly sliced
⅓ cup sliced almonds

1 Bring a large pot of water to a boil. Add 1 Tbsp salt, then the green beans, and cook until just tender, 3 to 4 minutes. Drain.

2 Meanwhile, heat the oil in a large skillet over medium heat. Add the garlic and cook, stirring, for 1 minute. Add the almonds and cook, stirring occasionally, until golden brown, 2 to 3 minutes.

3 Add the green beans to the skillet, season with ½ tsp salt and ¼ tsp pepper and cook, tossing until coated and heated through, about 2 minutes. Serve warm or at room temperature.

PER SERVING 99 CAL, 7 G FAT (1 G SAT FAT), 0 MG CHOL, 187 MG SOD, 3 G PRO, 8 G CAR, 3 G FIBER

Make ahead » Boil the beans until just tender, then plunge into a bowl of ice water to stop the cooking. Drain and refrigerate for up to 2 days. To reheat, add to the skillet with the toasted garlic and almonds and cook, tossing, until heated through.

Potato salad with celery and herbs

ACTIVE 25 MIN • **TOTAL** 30 MIN • **SERVES** 12
COST PER SERVING 45¢

3	lb red new potatoes
	Kosher salt and pepper
1	lemon
¼	cup olive oil
2	Tbsp Dijon mustard
4	stalks celery, very thinly sliced
¼	cup fresh flat-leaf parsley, chopped
¼	cup fresh dill, chopped
2	hard-boiled eggs, coarsely grated, for serving

❶ Place the potatoes in a large pot, cover with cold water and bring to a boil. Add 2 tsp salt, reduce heat and simmer until the potatoes are just tender, 12 to 15 minutes. Drain and run under cold water to cool. Cut the potatoes in half or quarter if large.

❷ Meanwhile, grate 2 tsp lemon zest into a large bowl, then squeeze in the juice (you should have about 3 Tbsp juice total). Whisk in the oil, mustard and ¼ tsp each salt and pepper.

❸ Add the potatoes and celery to the bowl and gently toss to coat. Fold in the parsley and dill and top with the eggs, if desired.

PER SERVING 153 CAL, 5 G FAT (1 G SAT FAT), 31 MG CHOL, 178 MG SOD, 4 G PRO, 22 G CAR, 2 G FIBER

Make ahead » Prepare the potato salad without the parsley and dill and refrigerate for up to 2 days. Fold in the herbs and top with the eggs, if using, just before serving.

Corn on the cob with chili salt

ACTIVE 10 MIN • **TOTAL** 10 MIN • **SERVES** 12
COST PER SERVING 76¢

12 ears corn, husks removed
4 tsp chili powder
   Kosher salt

1 Bring ot of water to a boil. Add the
co til just tender, 3 to 4 minutes.
 a serving platter.

 combine the chili powder
 he corn.

 ), 0 MG CHOL, 418 MG SOD,

> ***Love your leftovers »*** Make a zesty
> corn salad: Cut corn from the cob and toss the
> kernels with 1 tsp chili salt and 1 Tbsp each
> fresh lime juice and thinly sliced scallions.

Bulgur with creamy spiced carrots and raisins

ACTIVE 15 MIN • **TOTAL** 40 MIN • **SERVES** 6
COST PER SERVING 83¢

1	cup bulgur
	Kosher salt and pepper
⅓	cup nonfat Greek yogurt
1	tsp orange zest
3	Tbsp fresh orange juice
½	tsp ground cumin
2	medium carrots, coarsely grated
½	cup golden raisins
½	cup roughly chopped fresh cilantro

❶ In a small saucepan, combine the bulgur with 2 cups water. Bring to a boil, add ½ tsp salt, then reduce heat and simmer, covered, until tender, 12 to 15 minutes. Drain any excess water and fluff with a fork.

❷ Meanwhile, in a large bowl, whisk together the yogurt, orange zest, juice, cumin, ½ tsp salt and ¼ tsp pepper. Add the cooked bulgur and gently toss to coat. Fold in the carrots, raisins and cilantro.

PER SERVING 141 CAL, 0.5 G FAT (0 G SAT FAT), 0 MG CHOL, 315 MG SOD, 5 G PRO, 32 G CAR, 6 G FIBER

Switch it up » Replace the bulgur with another healthy whole grain. Cook 1 cup of barley, brown rice, farro, wheat berries or quinoa according to package directions, then follow the recipe as directed.

Smashed root vegetables

ACTIVE 20 MIN • **TOTAL** 45 MIN • **SERVES** 8 • **COST PER SERVING** 56¢

- ¼ lb (medium; about 3) parsnips, peeled
- 4 sprigs fresh rosemary
- 4 sprigs fresh flat-leaf parsley
- 6 cloves garlic, peeled and roughly chopped
- 1½ lb Yukon gold potatoes, peeled and cut into 1½-in. pieces
- 1½ lb (1 large) rutabaga, peeled and cut into 1-in. pieces
- ½ lb (medium; about 4) carrots, peeled and cut into 1-in. pieces
- Kosher salt and pepper
- ¼ cup olive oil
- Chopped fresh chives, for serving

Make ahead » Refrigerate the smashed vegetables for up to 2 days. To reheat, place in a double boiler or glass bowl set over (but not in) a pot of simmering water until heated through, 15 to 25 minutes. (Stir in extra warm water or olive oil if the mixture seems dry.)

1 Quarter the parsnips lengthwise. Cut out and discard the woody centers. Cut the remaining parsnips into 1-in. pieces. Using a piece of kitchen twine, tie the rosemary and parsley together.

2 Place the parsnips, herbs, garlic, potatoes, rutabaga and carrots in a large saucepan, cover with cold water and bring to a boil. Add 1 tsp salt, reduce heat, and simmer until the vegetables are tender, 12 to 15 minutes.

3 Remove and discard the herbs. Reserve ½ cup cooking liquid, drain the vegetables and return them to the pot. Drizzle the oil over the vegetables, season with ½ tsp each salt and pepper and, using the back of a fork or potato masher, smash the vegetables (adding some of the reserved liquid if the mixture seem dry). Sprinkle with the chives before serving, if desired.

♥ **PER SERVING** 182 CAL, 7 G FAT (1 G SAT FAT), 0 MG CHOL, 200 MG SOD, 3 G PRO, 28 G CAR, 5 G FIBER

Green salad with honey-lemon vinaigrette

ACTIVE 10 MIN • **TOTAL** 10 MIN • **SERVES** 8 •
COST PER SERVING 91¢

¼	cup olive oil
3	Tbsp fresh lemon juice
1	tsp Dijon mustard
1	tsp honey
	Kosher salt and pepper
2	shallots, finely chopped
2	heads green leaf or Boston lettuce, leaves torn (about 12 cups)
1	bunch radishes, thinly sliced
1	cup frozen peas, thawed
1	cup fresh dill sprigs

1 In a small bowl, whisk together the olive oil, lemon juice, mustard, honey, ½ tsp salt and ¼ tsp pepper; stir in the shallots.

2 In a large bowl, toss the lettuce, radishes, peas and dill. Toss with the vinaigrette just before serving.

PER SERVING 90 CAL, 7 G FAT (1 G SAT FAT), 0 MG CHOL, 154 MG SOD, 2 G PRO, 6 G CAR, 2 G FIBER

Cook's tip » Make a triple batch of vinaigrette. Refrigerate in a jar for up to 10 days. When ready to serve, let sit at room temperature for a couple of minutes before shaking and serving.

Barley with sautéed leeks, peas and parsley

ACTIVE 30 MIN • **TOTAL** 30 MIN • **SERVES** 6
COST PER SERVING 66¢

1	cup pearl barley
	Kosher salt and pepper
2	Tbsp olive oil
2	leeks (white and light green parts only), sliced into ½-in.-thick half moons
1	cup frozen peas, thawed
2	tsp grated lemon zest
½	cup chopped fresh flat-leaf parsley

1 In a medium saucepan, combine the barley, 3 cups water and ¼ tsp salt and bring to a boil. Reduce heat and simmer, covered, until the barley is tender, 20 to 25 minutes. Drain any excess water and transfer the barley to a large bowl.

2 Meanwhile, heat the oil in a medium skillet over medium heat. Add the leeks, season with ¼ tsp each salt and pepper and cook, stirring occasionally, until tender, 7 to 8 minutes. Add the peas and lemon zest and cook, stirring occasionally, until heated through, about 3 minutes; stir in the parsley. Fold the mixture into the barley.

♥ **PER SERVING** 195 CAL, 5 G FAT (1 G SAT FAT), 0 MG CHOL, 82 MG SOD, 5 G PRO, 34 G CAR, 7 G FIBER

Cook's tip » Barley is a great source of fiber. There are two types most commonly sold: whole grain (hulled) and pearl (the outer layer of bran has been removed), which cooks faster.

Broccolini with citrus vinaigrette

ACTIVE 15 MIN • **TOTAL** 15 MIN • **SERVES** 8
COST PER SERVING $1.30

3	bunches broccolini or 2 bunches broccoli
1	navel orange
¼	cup olive oil
6	cloves garlic, thinly sliced
¼	tsp crushed red pepper flakes
	Kosher salt

1 Fill a large saucepan with 1 in. water and fit with a steamer basket (or fill a large pot with ½ in. water). Bring to a simmer. Place the broccolini in the steamer basket or saucepan (if using broccoli, cut into large florets), cover, and steam until just tender, 3 to 5 minutes. Transfer the broccolini to a platter.

2 Meanwhile, using a vegetable peeler, remove 3 strips of orange zest; thinly slice the zest.

3 In a small saucepan, heat the oil, garlic and red pepper flakes over low heat until the garlic is just golden, 4 to 6 minutes. Transfer to a small bowl.

4 Squeeze 2 Tbsp orange juice into the bowl. Add the zest and ½ tsp salt and stir to combine. Spoon over the broccolini.

PER SERVING 118 CAL, 7 G FAT (1 G SAT FAT), 0 MG CHOL, 159 MG SOD, 5 G PRO, 10 G CAR, 2 G FIBER

Switch it up » The citrus vinaigrette is just as delicious on other vegetables. Try it on steamed green beans, roasted carrots or asparagus.

Tangy coleslaw

ACTIVE 15 MIN • **TOTAL** 15 MIN • **SERVES** 12 • COST PER SERVING 29¢

¾ cup lowfat sour cream

¼ cup fresh lime juice

1 Tbsp sugar

½ tsp hot sauce (such as Tabasco)

Kosher salt and pepper

1 medium head green cabbage (about 1½ lb green cabbage), quartered, cored and thinly sliced (about 8 cups total)

4 scallions, thinly sliced on a diagonal

1 large carrot, grated

1 cup golden raisins

1️⃣ In a large bowl, whisk together the sour cream, lime juice, sugar, hot sauce, ¾ tsp salt and ¼ tsp pepper.

2️⃣ Add the cabbage, scallions, carrot and raisins and toss to coat.

♥ **PER SERVING** 80 CAL, 1 G FAT (1 G SAT FAT), 3 MG CHOL, 147 MG SOD, 2 G PRO, 18 G CAR, 2 G FIBER

Make ahead » Refrigerate the coleslaw for up to 1 day. Toss well before serving.

Tomato and corn salad

ACTIVE 20 MIN • **TOTAL** 20 MIN • **SERVES** 12
COST PER SERVING 84¢

- 6 cups fresh corn kernels (from about 6 ears)
- 2 lb cherry or grape tomatoes, halved
- 4 scallions, thinly sliced
- 4 jalapeños, seeded and thinly sliced
- ¼ cup olive oil
- ¼ cup fresh lime juice
  Kosher salt and pepper

1 In a large bowl, toss together the corn, tomatoes, scallions, jalapeños, oil, lime juice, 1 tsp salt and ¼ tsp pepper.

♥ **PER SERVING** 120 CAL, 5 G FAT (1 G SAT FAT), 0 MG CHOL, 177 MG SOD, 3 G PRO, 18 G CAR, 3 G FIBER

Make ahead » Prepare the salad without the tomatoes and refrigerate for up to 1 day. Before serving, fold in the tomatoes.

Honey and lemon-glazed carrots

ACTIVE 15 MIN • **TOTAL** 25 MIN • **SERVES** 8
COST PER SERVING $1.05

3	lb medium carrots, sliced ¼ in. thick
¼	cup honey
2	Tbsp unsalted butter
1	½-in. piece fresh ginger, thinly sliced
	Kosher salt
1	Tbsp fresh lemon juice
	Chopped fresh flat-leaf parsley, for serving

1 In a large skillet, combine the carrots, honey, butter, ginger, ½ tsp salt and ¼ cup water.

2 Bring to a boil. Reduce heat and simmer, partially covered, stirring once, until the carrots are tender and the liquid has reduced to a glaze and coats the back of a spoon, 12 to 15 minutes. (If the carrots are tender before the liquid has thickened, uncover and simmer until the liquid forms a glaze.)

3 Stir in the lemon juice and cook for 2 minutes. Toss with parsley before serving, if desired.

PER SERVING 127 CAL, 5 G FAT (2 G SAT FAT), 8 MG CHOL, 239 MG SOD, 2 G PRO, 25 G CAR, 5 G FIBER

Switch it up » For a spiced up alternative, add 1½ tsp ground cumin along with the salt and finish with fresh cilantro instead of parsley.

Spice-roasted butternut squash and red onions

ACTIVE 45 MIN • **TOTAL** 15 MIN • **SERVES** 4 • COST PER SERVING 81¢

1 Tbsp light brown sugar

1 Tbsp ground cumin

½ tsp ground coriander

¼ tsp freshly grated or ground nutmeg

⅛ tsp cayenne pepper

Kosher salt

2 small butternut squash (about 2 lb each), peeled, seeded and cut into ½-in.-thick half-moons

2 small red onions, cut into ½-in.-thick wedges

10 sprigs fresh thyme

4 Tbsp olive oil

❶ Heat oven to 425°F. In a small bowl, combine the sugar, cumin, coriander, nutmeg, cayenne and ½ tsp salt.

❷ Divide the squash, onions and thyme between 2 large rimmed baking sheets. Toss the vegetables on each sheet with 2 Tbsp oil, then half the spice mixture.

❸ Arrange in a single layer and roast, turning once, until golden brown and tender, 25 to 30 minutes.

PER SERVING 325 CAL, 14 G FAT (2 G SAT FAT), 0 MG CHOL, 260 MG SOD, 4 G PRO, 52 G CAR, 7 G FIBER

Make ahead » Refrigerate the roasted squash and onions for up 1 day. To serve, bring the vegetables to room temperature, arrange on a baking sheet in a single layer and warm in a 375°F oven for 10 to 15 minutes.

Tomato, watermelon and arugula salad

ACTIVE 15 MIN • **TOTAL** 15 MIN • **SERVES** 4
COST PER SERVING $1.15

2	Tbsp fresh lemon juice
1	Tbsp olive oil
½	tsp honey
	Kosher salt and pepper
8	oz tomatoes, sliced
1	small jalapeño, seeded for less heat if desired, thinly sliced
½	small red onion, thinly sliced
12	oz watermelon, thinly sliced into 2½-in. pieces
2	cups baby arugula
½	cup fresh basil, roughly chopped (optional)
2	oz feta, broken into pieces

❶ In a large bowl, whisk together the lemon juice, oil, honey, ½ tsp salt and ¼ tsp pepper.

❷ Add the tomatoes, jalapeño and red onion and toss to combine. Gently toss with the watermelon, arugula and basil (if using) and top with the feta.

PER SERVING 114 CAL, 7 G FAT (2.5 G SAT FAT), 13 MG CHOL, 405 MG SOD, 3 G PRO, 12 G CAR, 2 G FIBER

Cook's tip » Fruit is a refreshing addition to summer salads. Try cantaloupe with tomatoes, fresh mozzarella and mint leaves or honeydew with arugula, thinly sliced shallots and a lemon vinaigrette.

Wild rice and cranberry dressing

ACTIVE 15 MIN • **TOTAL** 40 MIN • **SERVES** 8
COST PER SERVING 83¢

2	cups wild rice blend
¾	cup dried cranberries
2	Tbsp olive oil
2	large onions, chopped
	Kosher salt and pepper
2	cloves garlic, finely chopped
¾	cup fresh flat-leaf parsley, chopped
4	scallions, thinly sliced
¼	cup fresh dill, roughly chopped

1 Cook the rice blend according to package directions. Fold in the cranberries, cover, and let stand for 10 minutes.

2 Meanwhile, heat the oil in a large skillet over medium heat. Add the onions, season with ½ tsp salt and ¼ tsp pepper and cook, covered, stirring occasionally, for 6 minutes.

3 Uncover and cook, stirring occasionally, until the onions are very tender and beginning to turn golden brown, 4 to 5 minutes more. Add the garlic and cook, stirring, for 2 minutes; stir in the parsley.

4 Add the onion mixture, scallions and dill to the rice and toss to combine.

♥ **PER SERVING** 236 CAL, 0.5 G FAT (.5 G SAT FAT), 0 MG CHOL, 127 MG SOD, 4 G PRO, 49 G CAR, 5 G FIBER

Make ahead » Omit the scallions and dill. Refrigerate the rice mixture for up to 2 days. To serve, place the rice mixture in a large microwave-safe bowl. Sprinkle with water, cover and warm on high, stirring every minute, until heated through, about 4 minutes total. Stir in the scallions and dill.

p130

p146

p139

p152

Desserts

You don't have to skip treats!
These better-for-you cookies,
cakes and frozen goodies
will satisfy your sweet tooth.

Chocolate-cranberry pancake cake

ACTIVE 45 MIN • **TOTAL** 45 MIN • **SERVES** 10 • **COST PER SERVING** 54¢

3	cups all-purpose flour
1½	tsp baking powder
¾	tsp baking soda
¼	tsp kosher salt
3	cups buttermilk
5	large egg whites
1	large egg
2	Tbsp granulated sugar
1	tsp pure vanilla extract
1¼	cups semisweet chocolate chips
1	14-oz can jellied cranberry sauce
¾	cup sliced almonds, toasted
	Confectioners' sugar, for dusting

1 In a large bowl, whisk together the flour, baking powder, baking soda and salt.

2 In a medium bowl, whisk together the buttermilk, egg whites, egg, granulated sugar and vanilla. Add to the flour mixture and whisk until fully incorporated.

3 Heat a large nonstick skillet over medium heat. Add a heaping ½ cup of the batter, gently spreading it to form an 8-in. pancake. Cook until bubbles begin to appear around the edges and in the center, 1 to 2 minutes.

4 Flip the pancake and cook until the bottom is golden brown, 1 to 2 minutes more. Transfer to a paper towel set on a cooling rack. Repeat with the remaining batter, layering and stacking the pancakes between paper towels (you should have 10 pancakes total).

5 Melt the chocolate in the microwave according to package directions; set aside.

6 Arrange four 3-in.-wide strips of parchment or wax paper in a square around the edge of a serving plate (this will help keep the plate clean) and place one pancake on top of the plate.

7 Remove the cranberry sauce from the can in one piece. Slice in half lengthwise and place cut-side down on a cutting board. Cutting and placing one slice at a time on the pancake, cut 12 very thin slices from one of the cranberry sauce halves (you should get 30 slices from each half). Top with another pancake and spread it with 1 rounded Tbsp melted chocolate. Repeat the cranberry and chocolate layers 3 times. Top with a pancake, a final layer of 12 cranberry slices and the remaining pancake.

8 Spread the sides of the stack with the remaining chocolate. Gently press the almonds into the chocolate (use the parchment paper to help pat them on). Just before serving, dust the top of the cake with confectioners' sugar, then remove the parchment paper.

♥ PER SERVING 235 CAL, 6 G FAT (2 G SAT FAT), 13 MG CHOL, 200 MG SOD, 7 G PRO, 41 G CAR, 2 G FIBER

Switch it up » Replace the almonds with finely chopped roasted pistachios, toasted hazelnuts or pecans.

Banana oat cookies

ACTIVE 20 MIN • **TOTAL** 40 MIN • **MAKES** 3 DOZEN • **COST PER COOKIE** 11¢

1½ cups all-purpose flour
1 tsp baking powder
½ tsp baking soda
½ tsp ground cinnamon
½ tsp kosher salt
1 ripe medium banana
1 large egg
2 Tbsp canola oil
¾ cup packed light brown sugar
¼ cup granulated sugar
¼ cup unsweetened applesauce
2 tsp pure vanilla extract
1¾ cups old-fashioned oats
¾ cup dried cranberries
¾ cup pecans, chopped

1 Heat oven to 350°F. Line 2 baking sheets with parchment paper. In a large bowl, whisk together the flour, baking powder, baking soda, cinnamon and salt.

2 In a medium bowl, mash the banana. Add the egg, oil, brown and granulated sugars, applesauce and vanilla and whisk to combine. Gradually add the egg mixture to the flour mixture, stirring until just incorporated. Fold in the oats, cranberries and pecans.

3 Drop 1 Tbsp of the dough onto the prepared baking sheets, spacing them 2 in. apart. Bake, rotating the positions of the pans halfway through, until the cookies are light golden brown, 12 to 14 minutes. Let cool on the sheets for 5 minutes before transferring to wire racks to cool completely.

♥ **PER COOKIE** 88 CAL, 3 G FAT (0 G SAT FAT), 5 MG CHOL, 60 MG SOD, 1 G PRO, 15 G CAR, 1 G FIBER

Switch it up » Try sliced apricots and almonds or cherries and walnuts in place of the cranberries and pecans.

Mini black and white cookies

ACTIVE 40 MIN • **TOTAL** 1 HR • **MAKES** 5 DOZEN • **COST PER COOKIE** 5¢

1¼	cups all-purpose flour
¼	tsp baking soda
¼	tsp kosher salt
⅓	cup unsalted butter, at room temperature
½	cup granulated sugar
1	tsp pure vanilla extract
1	tsp lemon zest
1	large egg
½	cup sour cream
2	cups confectioners' sugar
2	Tbsp light corn syrup
3	Tbsp whole milk
3	Tbsp unsweetened cocoa

❶ Heat oven to 350°F. Line baking sheets with parchment paper. In a medium bowl, whisk together the flour, baking soda and salt.

❷ Using an electric mixer, beat the butter, granulated sugar, vanilla and lemon zest in a large bowl until light and fluffy, about 3 minutes. Beat in the egg. Reduce the mixer speed to low and alternately add the flour mixture and sour cream, mixing just until incorporated.

❸ Drop slightly rounded tsps of dough 2 in. apart onto prepared baking sheets and bake, rotating the position of the pans halfway through, until a wooden pick inserted in the center comes out clean, 6 to 8 minutes. Let cool on the sheet for 2 minutes, then transfer to a wire rack to cool completely. Repeat with the remaining dough.

❹ Meanwhile, in a medium bowl, whisk together the confectioners' sugar, corn syrup and 2 Tbsp milk until smooth and spreadable. Transfer ⅓ cup glaze to a small bowl and stir in the cocoa and remaining 1 Tbsp milk until smooth. (Icing should be thick, but spreadable. If necessary, add an extra ½ to 1 tsp milk.)

❺ Turn cookies flat-side up. Spread white icing over half of each cookie. Once the white icing has dried, spread chocolate icing over the other half. Let stand at room temperature until set.

♥ **PER COOKIE** 48 CAL, 2 G FAT (1 G SAT FAT), 7 MG CHOL, 17 MG SOD, 0 G PRO, 8 G CAR, 0 G FIBER

Make ahead » Store the cookies between sheets of wax paper in an airtight container for up to 2 weeks.

Red wine and spice-poached pears

ACTIVE 15 MIN • **TOTAL** 1 HR 10 MIN • **SERVES** 8 • **COST PER SERVING** $1.47

2   large navel oranges

1   750-ml bottle (about 3 cups)
    red wine (such as Merlot)

¾   cup granulated sugar

¼   cup packed dark brown sugar

¼   cup fresh lemon juice
    (from 1 to 2 lemons)

1   tsp pure vanilla extract

2   small cinnamon sticks

10 cloves

8   Bosc pears, peeled
    Whipped cream, for serving

❶ Using a vegetable peeler, remove six 1-in. strips of orange zest from the orange and place them into a large saucepan.

❷ Juice the oranges (you should get about 1 cup). Add the juice, wine, granulated and brown sugars, lemon juice, vanilla, cinnamon sticks and cloves to the saucepan and mix to combine.

❸ Add the pears to the liquid and bring to a boil. Reduce heat and simmer, turning the pears occasionally, until they are easily pierced with a knife, 20 to 25 minutes. Using a slotted spoon, transfer the pears to a platter.

❹ Remove and discard the zest and spices from the saucepan. Return the pan to the heat and simmer the liquid until syrupy and reduced by half, 25 to 30 minutes. Spoon the reduced sauce over the pears and serve with whipped cream, if desired.

♥ **PER SERVING** 232 CAL, 0 G FAT (0 G SAT FAT), 0 MG CHOL, 12 MG SOD, 1 G PRO, 58 G CAR, 6 G FIBER

Make ahead » Poach the pears 3 days ahead and refrigerate the reduced syrup. Warm just before serving.

Honeydew and mint ices

ACTIVE 25 MIN • **TOTAL** 25 MIN (PLUS FREEZING) • **SERVES** 12 • **COST PER SERVING** 34¢

- 1 3-lb ripe honeydew melon, cut into 2-in. pieces (about 6 cups)
- ¼ cup fresh lime juice
- ¼ cup granulated sugar
- ½ cup fresh mint leaves

❶ In a blender, purée the melon, lime juice and sugar until smooth. Add the mint and pulse until finely chopped.

❷ Pour the melon mixture into a 4½ x 8½-in. loaf pan or 1½-qt freezer-safe container. Cover and freeze until firm, at least 6 hours and up to 3 days.

❸ When ready to serve, let sit at room temperature for 5 minutes. Using a fork, scrape the surface of the melon ice to create flakes; divide among glasses or bowls.

....

♥ **PER SERVING** 38 CAL, 0 G FAT (0 G SAT FAT), 0 MG CHOL, 11 MG SOD, 0 G PRO, 10 G CAR, 1 G FIBER

> *Switch it up* » Replace the mint with thyme leaves and thinly sliced basil and add a pinch of salt to the mixture before dividing it among the glasses.

Melon pops

ACTIVE 20 MIN • **TOTAL** 15 MIN (PLUS FREEZING)
MAKES 10 ICE POPS (YIELD WILL VARY DEPENDING ON
ICE POP MOLDS) • **COST PER POP** 25¢

3	lb honeydew, cantaloupe or watermelon, rind removed, seeded and cut into 1-in. pieces (about 5 cups total)
2	Tbsp granulated sugar
	Ice pop molds (we used Cold Molds small)
10	wooden popsicle sticks

❶ Using a food processor, purée the melon and sugar until smooth.

❷ Divide the mixture among 10 ice pop molds. Insert sticks according to package directions and freeze overnight.

♥ **PER POP** 32 CAL, 0 G FAT (0 G SAT FAT), 0 MG CHOL, 11 MG SOD, 0 G PRO, 8 G CAR, 1 G FIBER

Flavor boost » Add thinly sliced strawberries or halved raspberries or blackberries to the mixture before freezing.

Baked Alaska

ACTIVE 35 MIN • **TOTAL** 1 HR 25 MIN (PLUS FREEZING) • **SERVES** 12 • **COST PER SERVING** 78¢

- 2 **pints raspberry sorbet, slightly softened**
- ½ **cup all-purpose flour**
- ½ **tsp baking powder**
- ¼ **tsp kosher salt**
- ½ **cup granulated sugar**
- 2 **large eggs**
- 2 **Tbsp canola oil**
- ½ **tsp pure almond extract**
- ½ **tsp cream of tartar**
- 3 **large egg whites**

❶ Line a medium metal bowl with plastic wrap, leaving a 4-in. overhang on all sides. Pack the sorbet into the bowl and smooth the top (it should be about 8-in. in diameter). Cover with the overhangs and freeze for at least 4 hours.

❷ Meanwhile, heat oven to 350°F. Oil an 8-in. cake pan and line the bottom with parchment; oil the parchment. In a medium bowl, whisk together the flour, baking powder, salt and 2 Tbsp sugar.

❸ Separate the whole eggs, placing the yolks in a large bowl and the egg whites in a separate bowl. Add the oil, almond extract and 2 Tbsp water to the yolks and whisk until fully incorporated. Add the flour mixture, whisking until the batter is smooth.

❹ Using an electric mixer, beat the 2 egg whites and ¼ tsp cream of tartar until foamy. Gradually add 2 Tbsp sugar and beat until stiff, glossy peaks form, about 2 minutes.

❺ Stir ⅓ of the egg white mixture into the batter, then gently fold in the rest (making sure that the whites are fully incorporated). Scrape the batter into the prepared pan and bake until a pick inserted in the center comes out clean, 20 to 22 minutes. Let the cake cool completely in the pan.

❻ Invert the cake onto a parchment-lined baking sheet. Uncover the sorbet and invert onto the cake. Remove the bowl (but not the plastic) and freeze for 15 minutes.

❼ Meanwhile, heat oven to 450°F. In a large metal or glass bowl, whisk together the remaining 3 egg whites, ¼ cup sugar and ¼ tsp cream of tartar. Set the bowl over (but not in) a saucepan of simmering water and cook, whisking constantly, until the sugar dissolves and the whites are very warm to the touch, 3 to 4 minutes. Remove the bowl from heat and, using an electric mixer, beat on low speed, gradually increasing to high, until soft, glossy peaks form, about 5 minutes.

❽ Remove the plastic wrap from the sorbet. Spoon the meringue over the sorbet and cake, swirling decoratively and making sure to cover entirely. Bake until the meringue just starts to brown, 3 to 4 minutes. Remove from oven, transfer to a serving platter, and serve immediately or return to freezer for up to 4 hours.

PER SERVING 169 CAL, 3 G FAT (0 G SAT FAT), 31 MG CHOL, 81 MG SOD, 2 G PRO, 33 G CAR, 1 G FIBER

Make ahead » Store the cake layer at room temperature and freeze the molded sorbet for up to 3 days.

Ginger crinkles

ACTIVE 30 MIN • **TOTAL** 1 HR 30 MIN • **MAKES** 6 DOZEN • **COST PER COOKIE** 4¢

2¾	cups all-purpose flour
1	tsp baking powder
1	tsp baking soda
¼	tsp kosher salt
¾	cup (1½ sticks) unsalted butter, at room temperature
1½	cups granulated sugar
1	large egg
¼	cup molasses
1	Tbsp fresh grated ginger

❶ Heat oven to 350°F. Line baking sheets with parchment paper. In a medium bowl, whisk together the flour, baking powder, baking soda and salt.

❷ Using an electric mixer, beat the butter and 1 cup sugar in a large bowl until light and fluffy, about 3 minutes. Beat in the egg, molasses and ginger. Reduce the mixer speed to low and gradually add the flour mixture, mixing until just incorporated (the dough will be soft). Refrigerate until firm enough to handle, about 1 hour.

❸ Place the remaining ½ cup sugar in a small bowl. Roll half the dough into 1-in. balls (about 1 rounded tsp each) and then roll in the sugar to coat. Place the balls on the prepared baking sheets, spacing them 2 in. apart.

❹ Bake, rotating the position of the pans halfway through, until cookies are puffed, cracked and set, 8 to 10 minutes. Let cool on the sheet for 2 minutes, then transfer to a wire rack to cool completely. Repeat with the remaining dough.

....

PER COOKIE 55 CAL, 2 G FAT (1 G SAT FAT), 8 MG CHOL, 31 MG SOD, 1 G PRO, 9 G CAR, 0 G FIBER

Switch it up » For an extra sweet treat, sandwich two cookies around frozen yogurt.

No-bake peanut butter crunch bars

ACTIVE 20 MIN • **TOTAL** 1 HR 20 MIN • **MAKES** 24 • **COST PER BAR** 34¢

4 cups whole-grain flake cereal, slightly crushed (about 2 cups)

2 cups whole-grain puffed rice cereal

1 cup dried cranberries

½ cup unsalted roasted peanuts

½ cup reduced-fat creamy peanut butter

½ cup packed light-brown sugar

½ cup honey

1 Tbsp unsalted butter

1 Line a 13 x 9-in. baking pan with nonstick foil, leaving a 2 in. overhang on the long sides.

2 In a large bowl, combine the cereals, cranberries and peanuts.

3 In a medium saucepan, combine the peanut butter, sugar, honey and butter. Stirring constantly, bring the mixture to a boil; simmer for 1 minute.

4 Immediately scrape into the cereal mixture and mix to coat. Lightly coat a spatula with oil or cooking spray and spread the mixture into the prepared pan, gently pressing it together and into the pan. Refrigerate until firm, 45 to 60 minutes.

5 Using the foil overhangs, transfer the entire bar to a cutting board and cut into bars.

♥ **PER SERVING** 129 CAL, 4 G FAT (1 G SAT FAT), 1 MG CHOL, 58 MG SOD, 3 G PRO, 23 G CAR, 1 G FIBER

Make ahead » Store the cut bars between sheets of parchment or wax paper in an airtight container for up to 1 week.

Grilled peaches with frozen yogurt and raspberry sauce

ACTIVE 20 MIN • **TOTAL** 20 MIN • **SERVES** 6 • **COST PER SERVING** $1.47

1 cup fresh or frozen raspberries (thawed, if frozen)

3 Tbsp granulated sugar

1 Tbsp canola oil

6 peaches or nectarines

2 cups lowfat frozen yogurt

1 In a food processor or blender, purée the raspberries, any juices and the sugar until smooth. Strain through a fine sieve. Cover and refrigerate the sauce for up to 5 days.

2 Heat grill to medium-high. Clean the grill, then lightly oil. Cut the peaches in half and grill until lightly charred, 1 to 2 minutes; transfer to bowls.

3 Top with frozen yogurt and drizzle with the raspberry sauce.

PER SERVING 222 CAL, 4.5 G FAT (1.5 G SAT FAT), 25 MG CHOL, 81 MG SOD, 10 G PRO, 39 G CAR, 3 G FIBER

Switch it up » The grilled peaches are also delicious with coconut sorbet, strawberry frozen yogurt or even just vanilla yogurt.

Chocolate-dipped coffee meringues

ACTIVE 25 MIN • **TOTAL** 1 HR 10 MIN • **MAKES** 8 DOZEN • **COST PER MERINGUE** 2¢

¼ cup granulated sugar
1 Tbsp instant espresso powder
⅛ tsp cream of tartar
2 large egg whites
4 oz bittersweet chocolate, coarsely chopped

❶ Heat oven to 200°F. Line baking sheets with parchment paper.

❷ In a large metal or glass bowl, whisk together the sugar, espresso powder and cream of tartar; whisk in the egg whites. Set the bowl over (but not in) a saucepan of simmering water; cook, whisking constantly, until the sugar is dissolved and the whites are very warm to the touch, 2 to 3 minutes.

❸ Remove from heat and, using an electric mixer, beat on low speed, gradually increasing the speed to high, until soft, glossy peaks form, about 5 minutes.

❹ Spoon the egg white mixture into a pastry bag fitted with a ¾-in. star tip. Pipe stars (about 1 in. wide) onto the prepared baking sheets and bake until the meringues are just set on the outside, 25 to 30 minutes.

❺ Slide the sheets of parchment paper onto wire racks and let the meringues cool completely. Slide a spatula underneath meringues to release.

❻ Melt the chocolate in the microwave according to package directions. Dip the tops of the meringues into the melted chocolate, letting any excess drip off, then transfer to the parchment to let set, about 20 minutes.

♥ **PER MERINGUE** 8 CAL, 0 G FAT (0 G SAT FAT), 0 MG CHOL, 1 MG SOD, 0 G PRO, 1 G CAR, 0 G FIBER

Prep tip » To keep parchment in place when piping, place a small dab of the egg white mixture on the corners of the baking sheet, then lay the parchment paper on top.

Stained glass cookies

ACTIVE 50 MIN • **TOTAL** 3 HR • **MAKES** 11 DOZEN • **COST PER COOKIE** 4¢

2½ cups all-purpose flour

½ tsp baking powder

¼ tsp kosher salt

¾ cup (1½ sticks) unsalted butter, at room temperature

¾ cup granulated sugar

2 Tbsp fresh lime juice

1 large egg

16 hard candies, assorted colors (such as Jolly Ranchers, sour balls or Life Savers), each color finely crushed separately

3½- in. ornament-shaped cookie cutters

1- to 1½-in. assorted shaped cookie cutters

1 In a medium bowl, whisk together the flour, baking powder and salt.

2 Using an electric mixer, beat the butter, sugar and lime juice in a large bowl until light and fluffy, about 3 minutes. Beat in the egg. Reduce the mixer speed to low and gradually add the flour mixture, mixing until just incorporated. Divide the dough in half, shape into two ½-in.-thick disks, wrap in plastic and refrigerate until firm, about 1½ hours and up to 4 days.

3 Heat oven to 350°F. Line baking sheets with parchment paper. On a lightly floured surface, roll out 1 disk of dough to ¼-in. thick. Using large floured cookie cutters, cut out cookies and transfer to the prepared baking sheets, spacing them 1 in. apart. Using smaller cutters, cut out the center from each cookie. Reroll, chill and cut the scraps.

4 Spoon about ¼ tsp crushed candy into centers of each cookie; brush off stray pieces. Bake, rotating the position of the pans halfway through, until the candy has melted and the cookies are lightly golden brown around the edges, 8 to 10 minutes. Let cool on the sheet for 5 minutes, then transfer to a wire rack to cool completely.

♥ **PER COOKIE** 35 CAL, 1 G FAT (1 G SAT FAT), 6 MG CHOL, 8 MG SOD, 0 G PRO, 5 G CAR, 0 G FIBER

Prep tip » To finely crush hard candies, place them in a freezer-safe resealable bag and pound with a meat mallet or clean hammer. Or use a food processor (clean and thoroughly dry between colors).

Apricot and pistachio cornmeal biscotti

ACTIVE 35 MIN • **TOTAL** 1 HR 20 MIN • **MAKES** 7 DOZEN • **COST PER COOKIE** 10¢

- 2 cups all-purpose flour
- ½ cup cornmeal
- ½ tsp baking powder
- ½ tsp kosher salt
- 4 Tbsp canola oil
- 1 cup granulated sugar
- 2 large eggs
- 2 tsp pure vanilla extract
- 2 tsp orange zest
- 1 cup pistachios
- 1 cup dried apricots, thinly sliced

❶ Heat oven to 350°F. Line baking sheets with parchment paper. In a medium bowl, whisk together the flour, cornmeal, baking powder and salt.

❷ Using an electric mixer, combine the oil, sugar, eggs, vanilla and orange zest in a large bowl. Gradually add the flour mixture, mixing until fully incorporated (the dough will be very stiff). Fold in the pistachios and apricots.

❸ Divide the dough into 6 portions and, with floured hands, roll each portion into a 1½-in.-thick log (about 6 in. long). Place on the prepared baking sheets and slightly flatten the tops. Bake, rotating the positions of the pans halfway through, until light golden brown and the tops begin to crack, 30 to 40 minutes. Let the logs cool for 15 minutes.

❹ Using a serrated knife, cut the logs on a slight diagonal into ¼-in.-thick slices. Arrange the slices on the same baking sheets in a single layer and bake until lightly golden, 10 to 12 minutes more. Transfer to a rack to cool.

♥ **PER COOKIE** 44 CAL, 1 G FAT (0 G SAT FAT), 4 MG CHOL, 17 MG SOD, 1 G PRO, 7 G CAR, 0 G FIBER

Make ahead » Store the cookies in an airtight container at room temperature for up to 2 weeks.

MEASUREMENT CONVERSION CHART

pinch/dash	⅟₁₆ teaspoon		
1 teaspoon			
½ Tablespoon	1½ teaspoons	¼ fl oz	7.5 ml
1 Tablespoon	3 teaspoons	½ fl oz	15 ml
¼ cup	4 Tablespoons	2 fl oz	60 ml
⅓ cup	5 Tablespoons + 1 teaspoon	2½ fl oz	75 ml
½ cup	8 Tablespoons	4 fl oz	120 ml
⅔ cup	10 Tablespoons + 2 teaspoons	5 fl oz	150 ml
¾ cup	12 Tablespoons	6 fl oz	180 ml
1 cup	16 Tablespoons or ½ pint	8 fl oz	240 ml
1 pint	2 cups	16 fl oz	475 ml
1 quart	2 pints or 4 cups	32 fl oz	945 ml
1 gallon	4 quarts or 16 cups	128 fl oz	3.8 liters
1 pound	16 ounces		

WHEN IS IT DONE?

The most accurate way to tell when meat and poultry are done is to use an instant-read thermometer. To the right lists the *Woman's Day* test kitchen's preference (and considered safe by many food experts and chefs) for tender and juicy results.

* The U.S. Department of Agriculture recommends cooking beef, pork and lamb to a minimum internal temperature of 145°F and poultry to 165°F for maximum food safety.

BEEF	WD TEST KITCHEN
Rare	118°F*
Medium-rare	125°F–130°F*
Medium	135°F–140°F*
Medium-well	150°F
Well-done	155°F

LAMB	
Medium-rare	125°F–130°F*
Medium	140°F*
Medium-well	150°F
Well-done	155°F

PORK	
	145°F

POULTRY	
White Meat	160°F*
Dark Meat	165°F

TEMPERATURE CONVERSION CHART

°F	°C
225°F	110°C
250°F	125°C
275°F	135°C
300°F	150°C
325°F	160°C
350°F	175°C
375°F	190°C
400°F	200°C
425°F	220°C
450°F	230°C

♥ For the nutritional criteria that make our recipes heart-healthy go to *womansday.com/hhcriteria*.

GENERAL INDEX

INDEX BY CATEGORY

ACKNOWLEDGEMENTS

There are so many steps that go into producing the recipes you see in these pages and so many people who are integral to their success.

Special thanks to the those who worked together to come up with ideas and develop recipes. And to those who joined us in the test kitchen tweaking and adjusting to ensure each recipe's ease and deliciousness: Anna Helm Baxter, Janine Desiderio, Alison Fishman, Jessica Goldman Foung, Mimi Freud, Jo Keohane, Donna Meadow, Brett Regot, Yasmin Sabir, Hadas Smirnoff, Art Smith, Chelsea Zimmer, Paula Zsiray.

Thank you to the teams that came together for photo shoots. Along with photographers, these food stylists, prop stylists and art directors help make our food look as good as it tastes: Isabel Abdai, Alison Attenborough, Christine Albano, Simon Andrews, Anna Helm Baxter, Roscoe Betsill, Frances Boswell, Stephana Bottom, Philippa Brathwaite, Cindy Diprima, Anne Disrude, Molly Fitzsimons, Matthew Gleason, Victoria Granoff, Megan Hedgpeth, Paige Hicks, Vivian Liu, Elizabeth Maclennan, Marina Malchin, Cyd McDowell, Donna Meadow, Frank Mentesana, Pam Morris, Elizabeth Press, Carrie Purcell, Maggie Ruggiero, Pamela Duncan Silver, Susan Sugarman, Erin Swift, Victor Thompson, Alistair Turnbull, Gerri Williams, Amy Wilson, Amy Wilson, Michelle Wong.

PHOTO CREDITS

Lucas Allen 8
Antonis Achilleos 40, 64, 70
Iain Bagwell 16, 17
Steve Giralt 4, 10, 26, 32, 44, 87, 88, 100, 102, 124
Raymond Hom 48
Lisa Hubbard 148
Yunhee Kim 22, 23, 77, 78
Charles Masters 104, 114
Johnny Miller 126, 130
Kana Okada 10, 18, 42, 72, 92, 128, 144
Con Poulos 4, 10, 34, 36, 47, 52, 58, 71, 78, 82, 90, 99, 104, 106, 108, 113, 121, 122, 125, 126, 132, 134, 139, 140, 142, 146, 150, 152
Tina Rupp 35, 112, 120
Kate Sears 4, 10, 28, 41, 46, 54, 64, 80
Kat Teutsch 12, 30, 38, 62, 66
Jonny Valiant 4, 20, 53, 56, 59, 60, 74, 76, 81, 84, 93, 96, 104, 110, 111, 117, 118, 136, 138
Michael Waring 7
Romulo Yanes 14, 24, 29, 50, 68, 86, 94

FRONT COVER
Kat Teutsch

BACK COVER
Kat Teutsch

HEARST BOOKS
New York

An Imprint of Sterling Publishing
387 Park Avenue South
New York, NY 10016

....

Editor-in-Chief Susan Spencer
Creative Director Sara Williams
Executive Editor Annemarie Conte
Food & Nutrition Director Kate Merker
Senior Associate Food Editor Yasmin Sabir
Associate Food Editor Anna Helm Baxter
Copy Editor Lauren Spencer

....

Book Designed By Victor Thompson

....

ISBN 978-1-61837-141-6

Distributed in Canada by Sterling Publishing
C/o Canadian Manda Group, 165 Dufferin Street
Toronto, Ontario, Canada M6K 3H6
Distributed in the United Kingdom by GMC Distribution Services
Castle Place, 166 High Street, Lewes, East Sussex, England BN7 1XU
Distributed in Australia by Capricorn Link (Australia) Pty. Ltd.
P.O. Box 704, Windsor, NSW 2756, Australia

For information about custom editions, special sales, and premium and corporate purchases, please contact Sterling Special Sales at 800-805-5489 or specialsales@sterlingpublishing.com.

Printed in China

2 4 6 8 10 9 7 5 3 1

www.sterlingpublishing.com